Anxious Kids *Anxious Parents*

Praise for *Anxious Kids, Anxious Parents*

"A very practical and straightforward approach to helping children learn to identify and deal with their anxiety. It has given me the tools I need to help my students and my own children. I've tried the strategies in my classroom with great success. The kids loved naming their anxiety and even drawing a picture of it. This helped them to externalize their anxiety and take control of it. Simply brilliant and very doable!"

Beth Lamb-Hamilton, teacher

"I have found the strategies very easy to implement on a daily basis. It is amazing how simple they are and how well they worked!"

Michelle Whalen, child and family counselor

"I implemented the seven steps with my daughter who suffers from separation anxiety. As a 'last resort' I reviewed the seven strategies and began to implement them. I am pleased and proud to say that as a family we developed a plan on how we were going to manage my daughter's separation anxiety and we stuck to the plan. I think the most important skill we learned was managing the worry instead of focusing on the reason for the worry."

DeAnna Renn, RN, mother and public health nurse

"This program is a simple yet very effective way to teach children and parents what anxiety is and how it works. It gives the family a common vocabulary when addressing anxiety that allows for better communication, better understanding, less frustration, and consequently, much success in empowering both the child and the parents in their pursuit to stop anxiety in its tracks. One of the best programs available!"

Manon Porelle, M.A.Ps., clinical child psychologist, Canada

"My son has difficulty staying overnight at people's houses. He even gets himself so worked up he ends up vomiting and thus the late night phone call to go and pick him up. By applying the principles, we decided to have a wake-over instead of a sleepover. I sent him with flashlights, books, and crayons, with the goal of staying up all night. The other parent even made a bet of who could stay awake the longest. My son won! He stayed up until 3 AM and had his first successful sleepover at a friend's house! Thanks, Lynn and Reid."

Lisa Clarke, mother

"Thank you to Reid Wilson and Lynn Lyons. I use their puzzle piece approach with both anxious kids and anxious parents. The approach really works if everyone works together."

Monette Boudreau, mother and teacher

"The strategies of not focusing on the content of the worry have helped immensely with my twelve-year-old son who has a generalized anxiety disorder. Having him recognize the anxiety for what it is has enabled us to focus on how to deal with worry in general, rather than frustrating ourselves with explanations and rationalizations about the specific content of a worry."

Susan Double, parent

Anxious Kids
Anxious Parents

7 *Ways to Stop the Worry Cycle and Raise Courageous & Independent Children*

REID WILSON, PHD *and* LYNN LYONS, LICSW

Health Communications, Inc.
Deerfield Beach, Florida

www.hcibooks.com

Library of Congress Cataloging-in-Publication Data

Wilson, Robert R. (Robert Reid)
  Anxious kids, anxious parents : 7 ways to stop the worry cycle and raise
courageous and independent children / Reid Wilson and Lynn Lyons.
    pages cm
  ISBN-13: 978-0-7573-1762-0 (Paperback)
  ISBN-10: 0-7573-1762-6 (Paperback)
  ISBN-13: 978-0-7573-1763-7 (ePub)
    1. Anxiety in children.   2. Worry in children.   3. Self-confidence in
children.   4. Parenting.   I. Lyons, Lynn.   II. Title.
  BF723.A5W55 2013
  155.4'1246—dc23

                                                                    2013028971

Publisher: Health Communications, Inc.
          3201 S.W. 15th Street
          Deerfield Beach, FL 33442–8190

Cover photo © iStockphoto
Cover and interior design by Lawna Patterson Oldfield

To my three guys,
Crawford, Brackett, and Zed,
and of course to my parents,
Ed and Cathleen Gerwig,
with love and appreciation
for everything

—Lynn

To Bob, Charlie, Michael, Matt, Jones,
Grayson, Mason, and Emma

—Reid

CONTENTS

INTRODUCTION

L et's face it: We parents are great at worrying about our kids. *How are they performing in school? Is she safe walking home from her friend's house? Should I limit his video gaming?*

And we are all so full of good advice, aren't we? "You had better start working on that paper before the weekend, because you've got that camping trip coming up." "When kids are mean to you on the playground, you just have to ignore them and walk away." "Five servings of fruits and vegetables a day. Let's put some color on that plate!"

But what happens when our sons and daughters start to show more than the average amount of hesitation about normal activities, expressing a degree of fearfulness that seems exaggerated for the circumstance? Suddenly, your son is afraid of anything to do with fire, and nightmares frighten him so that he doesn't want to close his eyes in bed unless you stay with him until long after he's asleep. Perhaps he has become more and more clingy and rarely allows you to be away from him. Is he no longer willing to play on the soccer team or perform in the school band, despite loving these activities in the past? How about spending the night at a friend's house? Has it become unthinkable?

Or maybe your daughter has slowly become reticent to go to school. It started out with her staying in bed past the alarm. Then stomachaches. Then more days when she felt "too sick" to go to school. And now, daily tantrums, fighting you every step of the way. Perhaps she was scared by an aggressive dog last year and still acts frightened every time she hears a dog bark. What loving, caring parent wouldn't become worried in the face of a child's anxious, avoidant behavior? So you offer your very best advice, logic, and encouragement, and nothing seems to help. It's not that you haven't tried the following:

- You reassure your son about the precautions you take to prevent any fire and how easy it is to call 911 if the rare event were to occur.
- You bring your daughter to the pediatrician, who assures her more than once that she's well enough for school. You even implement consequences for stalling in the mornings.
- You ask your daughter to come with you for a visit with your neighbor's dog, which doesn't have an aggressive bone in its body.
- You promise your teenage son that you'll keep your cell phone on while you're gone, and that you will come right home if he needs you.
- You remind your child of how much fun soccer was last year or how well his trumpet teacher thinks he's doing.
- You bribe your daughter if she will join you for a half hour at the park with her friend and mom.

Worry is exhausting for everybody. When anxiety is in charge, parents can feel like life is going in circles. You fix one problem (by handling the worry), and then another one pops up. It seems like there's no end to it.

We feel your pain, and we're here to rescue you from the cycle. We have spent our careers treating anxiety disorders. We have a combined fifty years of experience helping hundreds of families as well as school systems and communities support the development of courageous and independent children and teens. The advantage of studying and practicing one task for decades is that you can't help but get good at it. That's what we've been doing: figuring out what the science tells us about fear, worry, anxiety, and avoidance, and then what studies have shown us about how families can face challenges and step forward in spite of the threat. We have taken all we've learned from the research and from our own clinical experience and applied it to the skills we offer you here.

As parents ourselves, we know it isn't our job to stop worries from showing up, because they appear through all stages of life for *all* of us. Our children are going to worry, our teens are going to worry, and so are we. Our goal is not to prevent worries; it is to keep anxious fears from dominating our families. We've mastered some excellent strategies to help parents help their kids enjoy life again, and we give them to you in this book.

Here's a fact you might find surprising. Research shows that anxious children can learn patterns of worry from parents who are only trying to help. Our most common responses to our scared and worried children can end up encouraging them to remain frightened. When we act as worried, frustrated parents, we rarely teach our kids and teens how to stop being worried. Instead, we inadvertently teach them to think and act in ways that reinforce their fear and avoidance. What are some of the most common mistakes we might make?

- We try to convince kids that nothing bad is going to happen, that they don't need to worry because they are safe.
- We try to reassure them by overdetailing our schedules or the exact nature of upcoming events.

- We tell them everything will be fine if they just *calm down*, and we encourage them to learn skills of relaxation.
- We alter the family's plans and school activities to accommodate their fear and keep them comfortable.
- We excuse tantrums and outbursts of anger, as though they are an extension of the child's uncontrollable anxiety.
- We allow them to see our own anxious behaviors without role modeling any coping strategies.
- We become frustrated and angry and make unreasonable demands for our fearful child to "just do it."

In this book we explain the problems with all these approaches and teach you alternative ways to address your child's avoidance. Kids and teens *must* be in charge of pushing past their hesitations and into the wonderful adventures coming up in their future. They need a plan. Then they need to make it into their *own* plans. **You can't force them, and they don't like to be bossed around. But you can partner with your child to turn things around.** Here is an example of how things can change for the better:

***

Casey was an anxious, avoidant worrier throughout her childhood. Little signs showed up before kindergarten, as she was shy around other kids and adults. In the first couple years of elementary school, she was afraid of birthday parties, so her mom stayed at the parties with her. They skipped the Fourth of July fireworks at the park each summer—just too scary. If she went to the movies, she sat in the aisle seat in case she felt like she had to leave. All that careful avoiding seemed to work because it kept her from crying, shaking, and yelling.

By second grade, her mother was pleading with her to get out of bed for school in the morning, and Casey cried when it was time to leave for the bus. Soon, her mom started driving her to school as the only way to calm her down. Then Casey started refusing to get out of the car. She would cry, yell, and beg her mother to bring her back home. On the days she went to class, she often ended up in the nurse's office with a stomachache.

Missing class meant that she began to fall behind the other kids in math and spelling, which caused even more trouble, because nothing short of perfect was good enough for Casey. She sat at the kitchen table at night, sometimes for hours, making sure every letter of every word on her paper was flawless. She checked her math problems over and over. If she didn't understand a concept, she cried and yelled at her mother. In Casey's way of thinking, if she wasn't perfect, then it was a sign that either she was stupid or she was going to get in trouble with the teacher. In her words years later, "My worries took up far too much of my time and energy. I felt like worry was my companion, whether I liked it or not. We hung out together." No reassurances removed her doubts.

The last big trauma happened the evening of her holiday chorus recital in fourth grade. She was sitting on the bed, wearing her new green dress and letting her mom braid her hair. She felt nervous but really wanted to go. "Plus, after the recital," Casey said, "my friends and I were planning to go out for ice cream with our families. Who wants to miss that?"

Suddenly, Casey threw up. That was the first time her nervousness caused her to vomit. She missed the recital and missed the ice cream party. She cried herself to sleep, and she and her mom cried together the next morning. And that was the last day worry dominated her life. Casey put it this way: "As we talked, our tears stopped. And we both started to get mad. We decided then and there that we were going to treat this worry thing as a puzzle. And we were going to solve it!"

At fourteen, Casey has transformed herself from that anxious worrier into the normal, outgoing kid she is today. She hangs out with her friends, especially Shannon. This spring she had a blast working on the backstage crew for the school musical. And these last two seasons she's run on her middle school cross-country team. She's not the fastest member of the squad, but she has fun and feels accomplished.

Casey is a composite of the young people we have coached in therapy who, together with their families, have learned to beat anxiety at its own game. Your family can do this, too. We guide you in three ways:

1. We detail how worry tends to take control of a child's life (and yours!) and how families unknowingly adopt patterns that make worry even stronger.
2. We explain how you can help your child develop the courage to get over worry, using a language your child can understand. We create a metaphor of seven puzzle

pieces that we assemble with you. When you look at the list, you might view some of the strategy as unorthodox. But when you put all the pieces into action, you have a way out of this trap of anxious worrying.

3. We give you the concrete tips and exercises you need to move in a new direction—one that pulls your family away from anxious worrying and moves you back into growing and experimenting and discovering. As you will read throughout this book, understanding worry is important, but *taking action* is the key to conquering worry.

Kids, teens, and grownups who worry tend to think and do the same things repeatedly. The trick is recognizing how worry works and having a different response to it.

Think of yourself as a coach. Kids have to do the work, but coaches play an important role on their team as they push past their uncertainty. Perhaps you'll talk every day about what to work on, or maybe you'll just be there as a quiet supporter who encourages and reminds.

In the first ten chapters, we provide you with six of seven pieces to solve the puzzle of worried, avoidant kids. In Chapter 12 we give you the final piece, which will explain how to use the other six pieces together in a workable plan. At the end of each chapter appears a section called Time to Take Action: Applying the Concepts, in which we guide you in step-by-step, nonthreatening ways to help develop the skills for parenting an anxious child or teen. We ask you to look at your own beliefs and the ways you might avoid uncomfortable situations, as well as how you may unknowingly be role modeling the wrong behaviors for your child. Most important, we provide suggestions for planting the seeds of change in your family and your child, as well as concrete ways you can role model courage and independence in your child's presence. We want you to feel encouraged and hopeful as you read the chapters of this book. But, just as important, we believe you need to actively engage in the process of change. While we make suggestions throughout each chapter, we offer some of our most important recommendations at the ends of the chapters. They include looking a little more deeply at these problems you face and even challenging some of the ways you currently think and act.

Another part of the Time to Take Action section is Plant the Seeds. This section gives you tips for introducing your child to the important concepts and skills of each chapter in a more casual, indirect way. Engaging your child in a conversation, pointing out a pattern, or telling a relevant story are helpful methods for engaging your child's interest. Think of this process as planting seeds into the fertile imagination of your child. Then in Chapter 11, we offer activities that you and your child can do together. That's where these seeds will take root.

Also in Time to Take Action is Model the Process. When it comes to social behaviors, children primarily learn by observing their parents and other significant adults. We want to take advantage of your powerful influence as a model; that is the focus of this section in each chapter.

Some chapters include a Just for Parents section, too. As you learn more about how anxiety and worry influence your thoughts and actions, you have a chance to strengthen your parenting skills by doing the exercises presented here.

If you follow our suggestions within the Time to Take Action sections, then by the time you reach Chapter 11, you will feel like a stronger parent with clear principles on how to support a courageous and independent child. At that point your child or teenager will become accustomed to some new ways of looking at the challenges of the outside world. Then comes the tough part: getting your child to buy into the game plan. You can do everything right, but if your child continues to refuse action, your family will be stuck.

We won't abandon you as you try to influence your child or teen. We have written a free e-book specifically for anxious kids, voiced through Casey's character as a strong and healthy fourteen-year-old.* Called *Playing with Anxiety: Casey's Guide for Teens and Kids*, it tells the story of how Casey and her mom discovered those same pieces of the worry puzzle and put them together to transform Casey's life. Casey models the courage it takes for a kid to win over worry, and she will coach your child on how to be a winner, too. Make sure you have read and worked on these first ten chapters before you introduce *Casey's Guide* to your child. Then in Chapter 11 we summarize each chapter of *Casey's Guide* and offer a list of discussion questions to help your child learn the principles that Casey presents. We also include activities—even some playful ones—that you and your child can do together that reinforce the skills of each puzzle piece. By the way, these questions and activities in Chapter 11 are more helpful for the younger ages. Teenagers, who are growing more independent, will prefer to read *Casey's Guide* on their own (which is a good sign!).

While we have written this book in a casual, relaxed style, don't let our lightness fool you. We stand behind these principles, and we firmly believe that they offer guidance for parents of children at least as young as eight years old all the way through teens ready to graduate from high school. We have taught this approach to hundreds of families whose children were diagnosed with any of the major anxiety disorders, including specific phobias, separation anxiety disorder and

---

*You may download a free copy of *Casey's Guide* at our website, www.PlayingWithAnxiety.com.

school phobias, generalized anxiety disorder, social anxiety, panic disorder, and obsessive-compulsive disorder. (We detail the nature of these disorders in Appendix A.) We are confident that this book can help your family, too, but you needn't go this alone. In Appendix B we list several national mental health organizations that can help you find someone close to you who specializes in treating childhood mental health disorders.

How Worry Moves In, How It Grows, and Why It Needs to Go

When Elizabeth and her mom arrive at the office for their first appointment, they both look tired. Elizabeth hasn't been sleeping well, and she's keeping her parents awake with her nightly worries. In order to call it a night, she demands that they have long conversations about what happened during the day and what might happen tomorrow. Anxiety has taken a toll on this family, and it's been going on for many years. They're overwhelmed by the demands of worry, and they don't know what to do.

This story is familiar. Kids and parents can feel demoralized if they believe "This has been going on all my life, and it pervades so many areas of my life. It is not changeable." Often, families cope with such symptoms by avoiding stressful activities. While backing away helps everyone be temporarily more relaxed, life overall becomes far too constricted.

Anxiety is a curious thing because it has figured out how to be overwhelming and simple at the same time. When you start learning about anxiety, you have a lot to sort through. Anxiety disorders come in several different classifications, and thousands of pages of research can help us understand where it comes from, what it does, and how it is best treated. But when you're in the middle of it, it feels huge and twisted, like a maze with high walls and tricky dead ends.

On the other hand, anxiety is not that complex. When you take a few steps back and look at the whole picture, the tactics of worry are often surprisingly easy to understand. Sure, the details vary from child to child and family to family, but worry follows a fairly consistent pattern. From a distance, you can see the traps, but you can also see the exits.

In this chapter we give you some information on the purpose of worry and fear. We want you and your child to understand the normal, often useful role that worry and fear play in our bodies and brains. Then we differentiate between normal and problematic worry. You may be relieved to learn that some of the feelings and sensations your child and you experience are actually well-designed adaptations. You might also recognize that your concerns about your child's anxious behavior are valid and really do need to be addressed. We hope that the information will boost your motivation and your confidence in realizing that you can make a difference.

So let's start with the role of fear. Take a moment to imagine a time in your life when you felt scared . . . and your body's response was normal or even helpful. Here's one: As Lynn was riding her bike last summer, she noticed a large dog tied to a tree in front of a house. She watched as the dog barked and growled and pulled at his collar, standing up on his back legs and lunging her way. Then his collar broke away. Suddenly he was free and barreling toward her. Instantly, Lynn began pedaling fast. Really fast. Her body focused on one important goal, and, as the dog drew closer, her heart and muscles and eyes and lungs all worked to escape. She did, thanks to a powerful fight-or-flight response that kicked in perfectly when she felt threatened and afraid.

Our fight-or-flight response is here to protect us, just as it protected Lynn from that dog. And it comes with a set of major changes within the body:

- Blood sugar level increases.
- Pupils dilate.
- Sweat glands perspire.
- Heart rate increases.
- Muscles tense.
- The amount of blood in the hands and feet is reduced, and blood flows to the head and trunk.

These normal, healthy, lifesaving changes occur in the body's physiology, produced by communication from the brain to the autonomic nervous system, the endocrine system, and the motor nerves of the skeletal muscles. When the brain receives word that a crisis is at hand, it flips on this emergency switch, and all systems react simultaneously and instantly.

But what if you don't understand why your body is reacting this way? Maybe you think it is wrong or dangerous to have these intense sensations of arousal. Suppose you believe that the challenge in front of you is too big, you can't handle it, and the consequences are going to be harsh. Then you become anxious, which exaggerates the fight-or-flight response:

- Your heart may skip a beat or beat irregularly.
- Your stomach may feel as though it's tied in knots.
- Your hands, arms, or legs may shake.

- You may have difficulty catching your breath.
- You may feel pains or tightness in your chest.
- Your jaw, neck, or shoulders may feel tight and stiff.
- Your mouth may become dry.
- You may have difficulty swallowing.
- Your hands and feet may feel cold, sweaty, or numb.
- You may get a headache.

Now imagine that you're just a kid experiencing these sensations for the first time. No wonder our children start avoiding situations that provoke this set of changes. They don't expect it, they don't understand it, they are frightened by it, and—whatever it takes—they want to get rid of it. That's one of the primary reasons kids worry: they are anticipating upcoming events that might make them feel out of control again. Once they begin worrying, they will look for ways to calm themselves down, and they have access to very few options.

One strategic response is to give you and your child more ways to respond to anxieties and the circumstances that provoke them. First, you and your child can learn to *understand* fear, anxiety, and worry instead of just being driven by them. Where do you start? Children need to hear that being afraid is okay and even right. Fear and anxiety are the primary protective mechanisms we have in common with all other mammals. We humans are *supposed* to worry. It helps us to stop and think about our actions, to back away from dangers, or to fight for our lives if necessary.

What about a situation that's not life-threatening? Your child might start out afraid to sleep over at a friend's house, but that fear quickly builds into a fear of the anxiety itself, and what it will do to her when she's awake, alone, and far from you.

Here's the shift: What if she begins to think, "Worry is a very powerful part of me that protects me when I need it."? And then she thinks, "But I'm not sure how to manage it. Maybe if I learn more about it, I'll have a better chance to control my feelings."

Old Message	New Message
"Worry is powerful, complex, and bad. Get rid of it."	*"Worry is a powerful part of me that protects me when needed."*

This strategy of valuing a process—worry and anxiety—that is causing so much suffering may seem unorthodox. But it *is* our strategy nonetheless, and we hope it becomes yours. Instead of criticizing the worrying and cajoling your child to stop worrying, your job is to reinforce the understanding that being scared is okay. You can gain rapport with your child by saying, "Of course you are scared. You're not sure if you're going to be able to handle the situation. It's perfectly natural to have worries." In later chapters we give you advice on what to say next. But you can *start* by saying, "You're *right* to be scared."

WHEN WORRY WEARS OUT ITS WELCOME

"Fine," you say. "Worry is a normal response and we should appreciate it. Then please tell me what's going on in my house, because it doesn't feel normal around here!" You're right, too. Even though the worry response has its place, it can easily overstep its usefulness. Worry becomes problematic just like any other pattern can when used in excess, in the wrong places, and at the wrong times.

Parents often ask us how to know when worry moves from normal to problematic, because many worries sound like the normal struggles of childhood and adolescence.

Growing up is full of new challenges and experiences, and insecurities are inevitable. *Will I know what to do in my new classroom? Will I embarrass myself again? Will I be able to handle this like other kids? Are my parents going to be safe? Will I make it at camp? What if I don't like it here?* These *are* normal worries of childhood, but when they linger, trouble ensues. When momentary hesitations become incessant worries, children become increasingly anxious and stop moving forward into life.

Earlier we said that anxiety is simple once you step back and look at the big picture. It's simple because anxiety is a method of seeking two experiences: *certainty* and *comfort*. The problem is that it wants these two outcomes *immediately* and *continually*, yet life is full of surprises and discomforts, big and small. Overly anxious children tire out adults because such youngsters demand to know everything and to feel comfortable, and they expect the adults in their lives to make that happen. When you can't know everything and ensure perpetual comfort, your children may have the following behaviors:

- They cling to you.
- They refuse to try new activities.
- They continually ask you for reassurance of their "what if" questions.
- They feel sick and complain of aches, pains, and nausea.
- They avoid school or cry or throw tantrums if you force them to go.
- They act shy and don't talk in class or around others.
- They worry about future or past events ("I will look stupid

reading this book report" or "Will I get married?" or "Did I make my best friend mad?" or "Something bad is going to happen to my family").

When children don't learn to manage their uncertainty and discomfort—and come to understand excessive worry as an accepted part of living—they begin to avoid, which works wonderfully—from worry's perspective. If a child is terrified to ride the bus and refuses so strongly that Mom drives him to school, then his fear is replaced with the comfort and certainty of Mom's car, with Mom in it. He feels safe but gets no practice handling his worries.

While avoiding seems like the perfect short-term solution, in the long-term the anxiety worsens and additional problems develop. Untreated anxiety in children is one of the greatest predictors of depression during the teen years and adulthood. Children who avoid school and new experiences miss out on valuable opportunities for social connection and may not develop the social skills needed to make their way in the world. Substance abuse is more likely as a way to deal with anxiety. School performance suffers, and young adults with anxiety have greater difficulty leaving home and living independently.

Anxiety is common. Research shows that up to 20 percent of children have a diagnosable anxiety disorder, and the number is rising. Even without a diagnosis, virtually all kids have experiences of worry as they grow up. Certain factors—such as genetics, temperament, and stressful life events—increase the risk of developing anxiety, and we'll discuss those in Chapter 2. In Chapter 3 we look at how anxious patterns are learned within the family.

We know how confusing an anxious child can be. You are not alone. Anxiety is the number-one reason that parents bring their children to mental health professionals. It's also the most treatable. Anxiety and worry are normal parts of a full life, with all of its challenges and uncertainties. You didn't get this far without some anxiety, did you? Neither did we. In our opinion, helping your child learn how to experience and manage that worry is one of the greatest gifts that a parent can offer.

TIME TO TAKE ACTION:
Applying the Concepts of Chapter One

This chapter has covered three themes that will form the foundation for the strategies we're going to teach you. First, we took some of the mystery out of anxiety; second, we showed you how anxiety and fear can be helpful and necessary; and then we let you know that *action*, not avoidance, is the key to success. These are the concepts we now want you to actively explore.

Plant the Seeds . . .
of Optimism and Action

1. Kids listen when parents talk to each other, especially when the child is the topic of conversation. Within earshot of your child, look for opportunities to talk to your partner or another adult about what you've learned in Chapter 1. Be optimistic and positive. Make comments like, "We're really figuring out how this anxiety thing operates!" or "I never thought about fear as being helpful to me sometimes. That makes me think I don't always have to get rid of it."

2. Talk to your child casually about how you each might actively address the worry issue. Let her know that you are reading this book, and share some of the new concepts. Introduce the ideas in a relaxed manner. Don't immediately impose any new protocol, telling your child how she now needs to think or behave. We want your child to be curious, not defensive.

3. Express your own curiosity about what's to come. Use action words. "I'm excited that we're going to learn what to *do* about worry." "I'm reading this book about anxiety, and I can't wait to *dive in* to the next chapter!" Remember, worry is all about *stop* and *avoid*. Plant the seeds of movement and discovery.

Model the Process . . .
of Managing "Normal" Worry

Take some time to notice your own tendencies to worry. Reflect on your own worry management skills. How do *you* handle stress? How have you reacted to your child's fears and symptoms? Many parents living in a family ruled by anxiety tell us they've lost track of where their child's anxiety stops and theirs begins. Chapter 3 addresses parenting styles and influences in greater detail, and we'll be specific about which parenting patterns may need your attention. Right now, though, we just want you to start observing. Consider asking a trusted friend (who is willing to be honest with you) about how you appear to handle stresses and the ways in which you may be modeling anxious behavior. Another set of eyes can be quite informative.

Nurture or Nature?
Either Way, You Have a Job to Do

***

He's always been a sensitive kid. I remember when he was just a baby, less than a year old. . . . If a friend leaned into the stroller, he would start wailing. It took him a long time to tolerate my mother holding him. Even a new toy would upset him. He calmed down by the time he was a toddler, but he stayed very shy. I remember him constantly hanging on to my leg, and starting preschool was a nightmare for us both. When he was in second grade, he couldn't fall asleep unless we sat with him in his bedroom or left the bedroom light on.

***

We routinely hear this story from parents. Often they are asking us to see a middle-schooler who is showing enough increased signs of anxiety that the parents need professional help. As we detailed in Chapter 1, anxiety is common in children and adolescents, with over 20 percent of young people experiencing clinically significant anxiety at some point in their development. Of course, such a large problem has inspired study after study over the years, as researchers strive to explain the whys, whos, and hows of anxiety. Why do some children do fine while others struggle so much more? Who is most at risk? What makes anxiety worse or better? Is it genetic? Environmental? What about the parents' influence?

In these next two chapters, we explain the factors impacting the development of anxiety. In this chapter we start with the role of genetics and temperament. Even if your child (and you!) have dipped into the temperamentally anxious gene pool, you can learn how to manage this tendency and respond with parenting strategies that prevent anxiety from taking over your family.

STARTING OFF VULNERABLE

Scientists have found neither an anxiety gene nor a single cause of anxiety in children. (They haven't found one for depression either.) But infants can come into this world with a genetic predisposition to be sensitive, emotional, fearful, and high-strung. They are biased to feeling distressed when faced with unfamiliar people or unexpected events.

Children born with such a high-reactive temperament—researchers also call it "behavioral inhibition"—rarely outgrow this tendency. Jerome Kagan, a Harvard psychology professor who began investigating this trend over thirty years ago, talks of "the long shadow of temperament." Fifteen to 20 percent of babies are prone to respond to novelty with restraint or withdrawal. In research settings, three-month-old babies are observed flailing their legs, arching their backs, and crying when they hear a new voice or see a new toy. As toddlers, these same children are shy and easily startled. In the early elementary school years, they continue to act shy in class and at social gatherings. They take longer to warm up to peers or adults. By age seven, almost half of them show outward signs of anxiety, like fear of thunder or darkness, or extreme shyness.

Once into their teenage years, they may have grown out of specific phobias. They might manage to hide their distress from others and appear relatively normal on the outside. But this tendency toward anxiety doesn't fade away; it converts into worry. Just under the surface, their subconscious brains are still scanning the environment, nervous about some vague or even nonexistent threat. It's not pure fear. They become more preoccupied with a generalized sense of dread about future events. Again and again they mentally loop through the latest threatening "what if" scenarios.

About two-thirds of these inhibited teens spend excessive time carefully planning their days and preparing for worst-case outcomes. *Will I get this project done on time, and what if I don't? Should I meet up with them, and what do I say? Am I going to make a difference in this world?* These questions are fine for an adolescent to ask. The problem is that a highly reactive teen *continually* poses such questions, generating gobs of distress and not feeling settled about the answers. That's the difference between exploring and suffering.

As we said in Chapter 1, an untreated anxiety disorder in childhood is one of the strongest predictors of later depression. Much of this risk stems from that shy, behaviorally inhibited style of hanging back, worrying, and avoiding. These behaviors limit a child's social interactions, which is a problem.

Think about it: When kids are young, parents help orchestrate playdates and birthday party invitations. Moms and dads know to include the shy children, often working hard to make sure no one is left out. But by middle school, friendships strengthen or wither based on kids' interactions and interests. The parents no longer call the shots and make up the guest lists. Parties become sleepovers, and kids meet and bond at outside activities. When children avoid, social skills and friendships suffer, and the lack of positive social connections is a significant reason that teens become depressed.

It shouldn't surprise you that children who have separation anxiety (the need to stay close to a parent or home) may be showing an early manifestation of panic disorder. Recent findings support this theory: Nearly half of adults with panic disorder report having had separation anxiety in childhood—all the more reason to keep reading!

TENDENCY, NOT DESTINY

So, even though there is no anxiety gene, temperament makes a difference. In fact, four significant long-term studies are now following behaviorally inhibited children through their lives, and their data so far is clear: less than 10 percent of children who have a high-reactive temperament become consistently high-spirited, worry-free eighteen-year-olds who like taking risks.

If the traits we describe here match those of your child, you needn't let out a fatalistic groan. An anxious temperament predicts what a child often *won't* become, but it does not predict what he *will* become. You, dear parent, have a lot to say about that. Just as previous research foretold the future patterns in children who start off anxious, the latest research shows us how to intervene, what to do differently, and how to teach the skills that might not come so naturally to you. How you model behaviors, how you help your child approach novel situations, and how you debrief the struggles of childhood become opportunities to influence your child's orientation toward the future. Most important to remember here is that being a worrier can be temporary and is definitely changeable.

ANXIOUS PARENTS, WORRIED KIDS

If you have an anxious child, does that mean you're an anxious parent? There's a good chance that at least one parent is anxious, but a few different parenting pathways may have led one or both of you here. The first is the temperament we've just described. Perhaps you and your own parents remember worry-filled phases of your childhood years. Maybe you had trouble acting independently or were afraid to try new activities. If you were a behaviorally inhibited child, your tendency may have become your destiny.

Maybe your own mother or father was anxious, showing you the world through a worried, fearful lens. Heredity plays a part, but anxiety is also learned and may be part of a long family tradition.

Traumas in your past might be influencing your parenting style. The world can be a harsh and scary place, and perhaps you know this firsthand. You want to protect your children from what you endured, and that's understandable. Because of your past, handling uncertainty and letting your child move into the world feels overwhelming and intolerable.

Or maybe you didn't start out anxious. You've always been pretty easygoing about things . . . until your anxious child started refusing and clinging and melting down. Not knowing what to do but hoping to make each day run smoother and easier, you adopted worry's strategies, too. Now you and your child are worried about the worry, anxious about anxiety, and stressed out.

The recipe for anxiety in a child is probably some parts inherited, some parts learned, a portion parenting—all stirred by experiences with peers. The skills we teach to handle it are the same, regardless of where it began, whose genes did what, or how it was reinforced. And as we look toward change, your approach to parenting is going to matter a lot. If you are prone to anxiety and worry, then paying attention to how you interact within your family is especially important. Without knowing it, anxious parents pass on subtle messages to children, implying that to hesitate and to act overly cautious are positive traits.

If You Are an Anxious Parent, Why?

- Genes and temperament
- Modeling from your parent
- Traumas in your past
- Difficulties solving your child's struggles

Yes, changing our ways can be tough. But we strongly believe that when parents understand their role in perpetuating an anxious response to life, they can then embrace new strategies to alter the pattern.

The current research of Golda Ginsburg and her colleagues at Johns Hopkins University confirms this. Their findings show that when a parent is diagnosed with an anxiety disorder, the children are up to *seven times more likely* to develop an anxiety disorder themselves. No surprise that up to 65 percent of children living with an anxious parent meet the criteria for an anxiety disorder. (Dr. Ginsburg also has some great news for us, which we get to in a few pages.)

Researchers Paula Barrett, PhD, and Marc de Rosnay, PhD, looked at the impact of parents' modeling on their children. Dr. Barrett asked anxious children (ages seven to fourteen) to come up with plans of action when faced with an ambiguous situation phrase such as "What would you do if . . . ?" The children then joined their parents and were asked to further discuss the same situation as a family and provide a final response. After the family discussions, the anxious children's plans of action became *significantly more avoidant*. (With nonanxious children, the family discussions actually reduced the child's tendency to avoid.) This study provided the first evidence of how parents enhance the avoidant responses of anxious children, bolstering the need for families to look at how they might be supporting an anxious style of thinking and avoiding.

Dr. de Rosnay studied what happens when babies watch their mothers interact with strangers. The researchers trained the mothers, who were not suffering from anxiety, on how to behave in either a nonanxious manner or a socially anxious manner. While the infants (ages twelve to fourteen months) observed, the mother interacted with a male stranger. After watching their mothers act in a socially anxious manner, the infants were significantly more fearful and avoidant with the stranger. If the infants were evaluated as having a high-fear temperament to begin with, they were even more avoidant after watching their moms behave in a socially anxious way.

These excellent research examples confirm what we therapists see in our work with families every day. Anxious children want to avoid, and parents often model and support this behavior. Why? Three reasons. First, they don't know what else to do. How do you force a screaming, crying kid to do *anything*?

Second, it works. In Chapter 1, we talked about the effectiveness of avoidance as a short-term strategy for handling anxiety. Remove or fix the immediate anxiety-provoking situation, and your child becomes less distressed. This short-term fix can quickly become the coping strategy of choice in families.

Why Parents Help Kids Avoid

- You don't know what else to do.
- It works. Anxious kids calm down.
- You want to protect your child.

Third, if you're anxious yourself, you may be even quicker to move in with solutions when your child is anxious, as you have a harder time recognizing or tolerating the normal anxiety of new experiences. When we talk to parents about helping their worried kids, we often hear the following reasons for jumping in to rescue. They are all based on a concern for a child's safety and a desire to protect and care for them. Do they sound familiar?

- I have anxiety myself, and I can't stand to see my child suffer like I do.
- I know how it feels, and I know how to make it stop.
- I believe that anxiety is dangerous. It could damage my child.
- I can't stand to see my child uncomfortable in any way.
- My child is fragile and can't be pushed.
- I'm the parent, so it's my responsibility to fix the situation.

Then there's the big one: "What else am I supposed to do?"

Again, we get it. As parents, we don't want our children to experience distress. But if you carry around these beliefs about anxiety and discomfort, you are likely acting in a way that reinforces your child's feelings of helplessness. By accommodating the anxiety and offering constant reassurances, you inadvertently encourage your child to become overly dependent on you. She will miss opportunities to develop her own problem-solving and coping skills. Every time you take over for your child or give her excessive attention when she's scared, you send the message that she can't handle difficulties and that her fears are justified.

Accommodating the child's need for comfort and reassuring the child that "everything will be fine" are the most common patterns we see in anxious as well as nonanxious parents. Kimberly's story illustrates one of the many forms such patterns can take:

✳ ✳ ✳

Kimberly was a bright, albeit stubborn, thirteen-year-old who was brought to therapy because her separation anxiety was driving her parents crazy. She wouldn't allow her mom to leave the house for even a few minutes without her and refused, for example, to go find the milk in the dairy section while her mom waited in the deli line at the grocery store. Kimberly, however, felt fine about the way she ordered everyone around. She kept her worry in check, as long as everyone else behaved accordingly.

We worked together on the puzzle pieces (the step-by-step strategies that we teach you starting in Chapter 4), and Kimberly was mildly cooperative but rather unenthusiastic. Who needs to go get the milk anyway? So we looked for a want-to—something that was important to her, a desired activity that would inspire her to move into unknown territory and take charge of her worry. In May, her eighth-grade class was going on a three-night trip to a camp about sixty miles away. Kimberly and her friends were excited. It was a traditional eighth-grade event at the school, marking the end of middle school.

Aha! Something Kimberly wanted! Now we could get somewhere. In preparation we talked about pushing through the uncertainty, about embracing each step along the way as she moved closer to the goal of participating in this fun event. Kimberly was clear: "I really want to go on the trip. I want to make it happen." It was going to be uncomfortable and new, but she seemed willing. Great! She made her list of steps and tools she would use to manage her worry, and off she went.

A few weeks later, Kimberly returned. She had gone on the trip, she said. Success! Mom's face, however, did not have a look of success. Not even close, actually.

"Well, she went on the trip," Mom said. "But she didn't stay overnight." Mom then revealed what can only be described as the stunning accommodations Mom, Dad, the grandparents, and the other siblings endured to make sure Kimberly (and her anxiety) got what she wanted. Imagine what it took for two working parents to bring a child sixty miles each way, morning and evening, for three days during the middle of a school week. Yes, that's an extra 240 miles of driving a day.

Kimberly sat smiling with her arms folded across her chest. Mom just looked tired. A few weeks later, Mom called to end therapy. "She's just not willing to make the changes she needs to make."

***

You must become aware of this pitfall. Kimberly's parents helped her accommodate her worried thoughts and feelings. No one in the family was willing to tolerate Kimberly's discomfort, which often looked very much like anger. As a result, she got what she wanted without having to take any difficult steps or practice the tools, because as soon as the anxiety and anger escalated, Mom and Dad did what they could to "help." Her desire to go to the camp was a great opportunity. Unfortunately, it only served to strengthen Kimberly's anxious, demanding approach to uncertainty. And it reinforced in everyone's mind that Kimberly wasn't capable of handling the situation.

Let's look at some of the common anxiety-driven patterns into which parents fall. You'll recognize many of them in Kimberly's story and in the other families we describe throughout the book. We're going to guess that you'll also recognize yourself somewhere on the list. These patterns feel intuitive and seem to make the problem recede quickly. You're stuck in these reactions because worry is exhausting and you haven't known what else to do. Hang in there. The skills we teach in the upcoming chapters target these tricky parent traps.

- *Rescuing, reassuring, and overprotecting.* When you step in to save your child, and when you provide constant reassurance that she's okay and capable, you prevent her from learning how to solve problems on her own. When you do all the talking, she doesn't learn to talk to herself in a way that promotes her ability to experiment and master new tasks.
- *Providing certainty.* Many parents give a worried child detailed descriptions about an upcoming event. Anxiety hates uncertainty, so parents give information about who will be at a party, where parents are at all times, what will be on the menu at a restaurant . . . which supports rigidity and teaches

children that they cannot move forward unless they know
everything in advance. What happens in your house when
plans unexpectedly change?

- *Identifying a child as a worrier because "it runs in the
family."* Parents who are anxious must be careful not to accept
the anxious family patterns as inevitable or purely genetic.
Anxiety can be a part of a child's or family's experience,
but too many families adopt it as their identity. Anxiety is
one of the most treatable disorders in all of mental health.
Suggestions that it is permanent and inevitable are inaccurate
and discouraging to children and parents.

- *Requiring family members, friends, and schools to
accommodate the anxiety.* Kimberly's family went to great
lengths to make sure she was able to participate on some level
in the school trip. Parents, grandparents, and siblings worked
hard to keep her comfortable while indirectly giving Kimberly
the message that her anxiety was in charge. It worked out
well for Kimberly and her desire for comfort, so it was not
surprising that she stopped coming to therapy.

- *Allowing "bad" behavior (yelling, swearing, tantrums,
hitting, etc.) because it's part of the anxiety.* Anger is
certainly common with anxious kids. "Fight" is within the
fight-or-flight response; if you've ever seen a trapped animal,
you know what we mean. This reaction is a sign that your
child does not have the skills to manage uncomfortable
emotions and will do what's necessary to avoid them.
Allowing your child to act in this way supports the control
that the anxiety has over everyone and ultimately impacts his
relationships with friends and family and at school. We have
also seen how quickly this behavior bleeds out into other areas

where anxiety is not really an issue. If a child discovers how effective anger can be to manage others, he will use it more freely. Assuming you don't allow this behavior with your other children, don't allow it with your anxious child either.

- *Modeling with your own anxious behavior.* Remember, kids pick up even the subtle cues of a parent's anxious behavior. You can imagine what they learn if they watch you drive with tension, struggle with panic attacks, worry out loud, or lose control when you're stressed.
- *Pushing too hard or becoming angry or explosive.* We know how frustrating anxiety can be, and most parents we talk to lose it on a regular basis. They also recognize it doesn't work. If you don't know how to swim, someone yelling "*Swim!*" at you won't help you master the freestyle.

All that said, by picking up this book you made an important decision to learn what you and your child can do differently. You might still feel frustrated as you move through this process, but when families understand anxiety and have a plan, the explosiveness that comes from feeling helpless decreases dramatically.

THE POWER OF POSITIVE ROLE MODELING

Earlier, we told you about Golda Ginsburg's research on the significant impact of parental anxiety on children, and we promised some better news. After Dr. Ginsburg and her colleagues at Johns Hopkins confirmed their suspicions that anxious parenting puts kids at risk for developing their own anxiety disorders, the researchers went about creating a program focused on preventing this pattern from continuing.

Common Parenting Patterns That Make Sense and *Don't Work*

- Rescuing, reassuring, and overprotecting
- Providing certainty
- Identifying a child as a worrier because "it runs in the family"
- Requiring family members, friends, and schools to accommodate the anxiety
- Allowing "bad" behavior (yelling, swearing, tantrums, hitting, etc.) because it's part of the anxiety
- Modeling with your own anxious behavior
- Pushing too hard or becoming angry or explosive

The Hopkins team studied forty children between seven and twelve years old not diagnosed with anxiety but known to have one or both parents diagnosed with an anxiety disorder. Half of the families were enrolled in an eight-week cognitive behavioral therapy program, while the other half were put on a waiting list and received no therapy during the time of the study. (They were able to receive the therapy a year later.)

The eight-session program, consisting of hour-long weekly sessions, helped parents change behaviors believed to contribute to anxiety in children, such as overprotection, excessive criticism, and unwarranted expression of fear and anxiety in front of the children. Meanwhile, the children learned how to manage anxiety-provoking situations and practiced new problem-solving and coping skills. Within a year, 30 percent of the children in the no-intervention group had developed an anxiety disorder, compared to *none* who participated in the family-based therapy groups.

This research is powerful. It supports what we know is possible and how important you are in this process. You can't do this *for* your child, but you are the critical coach and guide as your child learns these skills—and you must learn some skills, too. As a parent, you'll need to build your tolerance for doubt and helplessness and be able to forgive yourself for past mistakes. You should develop the same expectations of your anxious child as with your other children, with some modifications while she learns a new perspective. You need to give her the hope of recovery and the belief in her capacity to cope.

And One More Thing . . .

Some families include an anxious parent and a nonanxious one. The nonanxious parent is often a valuable—and untapped— resource and positive model. Unfortunately, too often we find that these nonanxious parents have stepped away from asserting themselves after being accused of being "too careless," "not worried enough," and getting blamed if something bad actually happens. The anxious members of the family tell them that they can't possibly understand and are actually causing harm by pushing the child into activities. We encourage these nonanxious parents to step back into the family to support and model the positive skills we teach.

TIME TO TAKE ACTION:
Applying the Concepts of Chapter 2

Just for Parents

1. Spend some time thinking about how worry might have been passed down in your family. What messages did your parents give to you as a child?

2. What coping strategies did your family use to handle worry, danger, or fear?

3. Were you shy as a child? A worrier? How did those traits influence your behavior and your sense of self?

4. Have you addressed your own anxiety?*

* In Appendix B, we list several resources to help adults learn how to handle their own anxiety, though certainly the tools described in this book can work for adults, too.

Plant the Seeds . . .
of Change on the Horizon

This chapter helps you to notice how you may be contributing to the worry in your family, either by your inevitable genetic contribution or by your sometimes desperate efforts to make the worry go away. Discovering how our actions as parents influence our children in a not-so-good way can be intimidating, but we hope such discovery also enlightens and motivates you.

• Talk casually about how worry has been bossing you around, too. Choose as examples situations that are normal and occur every day. We want you to show your child that worry is a normal part of life that can be handled, but please don't bring your child into the bigger worries of your adult life, like financial, health, or relationship problems. (Examples of "everyday" worries: "Sometimes when I want to just sit quietly, my worries about our busy week ahead start going a mile a minute." "I was worrying about what to get Grammie for her birthday because I wanted it to be the perfect gift, so I had a bit of trouble falling asleep last night.") Plant the seeds that you're going to start responding differently when worry shows up and that you're looking forward to handling the anxiety in a new way. Appendix C offers a list of wonderful children's books that address change and flexibility in creative ways. Many are available at libraries. Stories are a wonderful way to plant seeds and start conversations.

Model the Process . . .
of Positive Actions

The research we included in this chapter emphasizes the importance of adult role modeling in the development of children's coping styles. Isn't it amazing that even children as young as twelve months were immediately impacted by their mothers' responses to strangers? As you continue to read and learn, pay attention to what you say and how you react, not only to your child, but to the world around you. Knowing that your child is watching and listening means you have the power to make a big difference. As a starting point, pay attention to how many times you say, "Be careful!" to your child. What other phrases might you try instead? How about, "Think a few steps ahead" or "Use your head and have fun!"? Keep your ears open for phrases others use that give either a message of caution or a vote of confidence.

3

It Seemed Like a
Good Idea at the Time . . .

A friend told a story recently about her attempt to sell her seven-year-old on the "natural" alternative to Oreos, to which her child pointed out, "'Natural' on the label doesn't mean good or bad. Arsenic is natural, and so are rattlesnakes. Just because these cookies are natural doesn't mean they're better."

We can apply this same observation to anxiety and worry: Just because certain factors play a role in strengthening anxiety, they're not always negative. In fact, in this chapter you're going to discover how some of these influences can actually be helpful, productive, and even occasionally enjoyable. But in the world of anxiety, they often hijack your child and then the positive aspects are lost.

A few of these factors are internal—sensitivity to stimuli, imagination, high standards, perfectionism, and some are external—life events, other people's actions, and the world we live in. When the internal and external join together, which they often do, children without adequate coping strategies become overwhelmed.

For instance, a subset of kids can be more sensitive to loud noises, a hurried pace, and other stresses of daily life. While their friends might thrive on action video games blaring on the TV screen or the adrenaline rush of scary movies, these kids become anxious and tense. Eventually, such children learn to turn down invitations to those activities as the only way to manage their distress. Of course, reducing their social outlets makes them feel more isolated. Adding to that, they become disappointed in themselves for being bothered by small things that don't trouble their friends.

Imagine a child with a strong internal drive to succeed who ends up in the class of a demanding teacher, or a child with a vivid imagination who overhears a story about a house fire on the news and replays the scary scenario over and over in her head. Children without adequate coping skills become overwhelmed. Taking advantage of their vulnerability, anxiety and worry ramp up in a way that paralyzes them.

Not every child needs to enjoy aggressive video games, but you and your child need to develop the skills and coping mechanisms that give you the option for your child to engage in more challenging activities. Here we start thinking broadly about how we might respond to today's fast-paced life and the constant stimulus that we all face. Then we highlight two traits of anxious kids and parents that cause havoc in our plans.

"The World Is Too Much with Us"

The line above is the title of a poem written by William Wordsworth in 1802. More than 200 years ago the poet was expressing his dismay at the pace of the world and at humanity's movement away from the flow and rhythm of nature. He worried about our practice of "getting and spending." Rather prophetic. What would he think of shopping in a mall on Black Friday, or eating a meal in the car while rushing to make it from soccer practice to flute lessons?

We are stressed out. In general, we work too much, schedule too much, and hear about too many horrible events in the world. And our kids are watching.

A camp on a lake in New Hampshire maintains its tradition of no electronics available to the campers or their parents. No phone calls or e-mails. No computers or televisions. The children have the opportunity to write home every day after lunch, and every afternoon the mail boat arrives with letters and packages from family. The kids love it. There's a long waiting list to attend this camp, and every bunk has been filled every week of summer for as long as anyone can remember. The parents? Maybe some have a bit more trouble letting go these days. The camp director told us how a mother sewed a cell phone into her son's stuffed bear, unable to imagine that he could handle the disconnect.

We won't belabor this point. We know what life is like and how easy it is to get sucked into the demands and pace of it all. But as you read through the rest of the chapters and learn the skills, pay more attention to your family's schedules. The basics, like sleep and play and quiet time, are essential to everyone's well-being. If you have an anxious child, your job is to make sure that you have not become numb to the stressors of the external world, and that you tune in to the pace your family is keeping.

"Okay, wait a minute," you say. "Didn't you just warn me about being overprotective? What about the need to push my child into new territory?" Good question. And as clichéd as this answer sounds, it's about finding balance. Children need to explore and experiment and work through the nervousness of new situations. But pushing children *without first giving them the skills to cope and problem solve only leads to more resistance.*

Children need to be able to move forward without the voice of anxiety announcing that they can't handle what's in front of them. Does this mean they have to do everything? Of course not. Children and parents need to learn when it's important to move forward and when it's okay to say, "No, thanks." Should kids be required to go to scary movies? Not necessarily. But they do need to learn how to get through a test at school or sleep in their own beds or how to order in a restaurant or ask for directions when lost.

As parents, you need to learn when it's important to push and when to back off. Is your child expressing a preference, or is worry stepping in? You may already have a clear sense of when your child's anxiety is preaching avoidance, or you may only recognize anxiety's influence after the fact.

Anxiety is strengthened by two common internal processes: an *imagination* that focuses on the worst possible outcomes ("I know I'm going to get stung by that bee!") and *rigid perfectionism* ("It has to be done this way!"). These cognitive patterns make the unpredictable world around us even more overwhelming, so they need to be addressed. Explaining how these patterns work helps show why flexibility is essential to managing anxiety.

IMAGINE WHAT?

In the world of running, a four-minute mile was believed to be not only impossible but dangerous. It just couldn't be done, and this was considered fact . . . until 1954, when a twenty-one-year-old medical student named Roger Bannister ran the mile in 3 minutes, 59.4 seconds. Forty-six days later, another miler named John Landy ran an amazing 3:57.9. Later that year, Bannister and Landy raced each other. Bannister won, but again both finished under the "impossible" four-minute time. By the end of 1957, sixteen more runners had run sub-four-minute miles. The limiting belief in the impossibility of a four-minute mile—accepted as fact for decades— dramatically fell away.

Imaginations are powerful. They enable us to create and plan and discover. We can visually rehearse an activity, try out a new idea, or practice a skill, all safely inside our minds. We have the capacity to engage our imaginations to access pleasure, competence, pride, determination, creativity, and so many other useful states of mind. It is an essential part of how we learn to be successful.

Imaginations also have the capacity to make us vomit. Tremble. Scream. Lock the doors and hide in the closet. When we get absorbed in our imaginations, we create reactions in our bodies and develop beliefs that are sometimes amazing and sometimes destructive. What we allow our minds to envision and what we say to ourselves along the way have a great impact on what we feel and then what we do.

Anxious children, we have observed, have active imaginations, which is great . . . sort of. People who worry tend to have a cognitive pattern called "catastrophic thinking." Their thoughts travel quickly to the worst-case scenario. They hone in on the most negative of all possible outcomes. They begin a test with the presumption that they'll forget all the information they learned. Every plane flight ends in a fiery explosion. Every dog is going to bite.

Anticipating an event, then scaring ourselves, and then avoiding the event so that we're no longer scared can become a self-reinforcing pattern that is difficult to break. Imagine you have a child who has been invited to spend the night at a friend's house. While she would love to spend time with her friend, she begins to feel afraid that something bad might happen that she couldn't handle on her own. She begins to think, *What if I get really scared and I can't sleep? Or what if I have nightmares?* Simply anticipating the event, she starts feeling sensations of anxiety: her heart starts to race, her hands get clammy, and she gets a pain in the pit of her stomach. Now what is she thinking? *Boy, if I'm feeling this bad now, I can just imagine what it might be like at Joanna's house!* And she *does* imagine it, which causes her to become even more distressed. If she has no resources to manage her current distress—and believes she will have no resources to handle her distress in the middle of the night at Joanna's—that's intolerable for her. She decides to make up some excuse, or perhaps she asks you to make up an excuse for her. Then something interesting happens. She immediately feels better. It worked! Avoiding a distressing event makes her feel better. Since the assurance that she can stay at home is rewarded by physical comfort and emotional relief, she naturally and unconsciously seeks out that answer to her problem the next time it comes up. In other words, feeling relief in the last step can make the next cycle even more likely (see Figure 3.1).

We can replace "spend the night out" with any threatening event, and the pattern would look the same. It shows us how children's imaginations and worries lead to anxiety. When those sensations are intolerable, avoidance becomes the expected solution. Avoidance leads to relief, which then offers an easy answer for next time. With no other alternative to take away their distress, and since they cannot tolerate their sensations of anxiety, such children—sometimes stubbornly—refuse to participate.

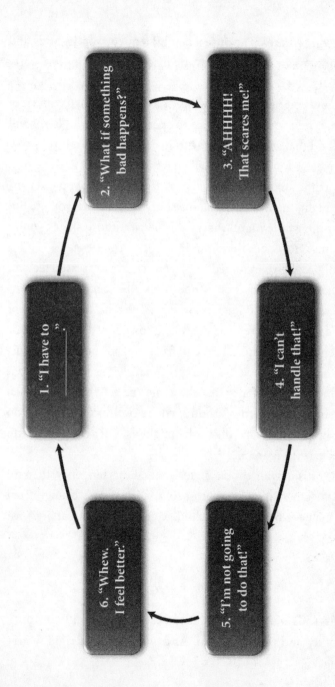

Figure 3.1: How Avoidance Strengthens Worry

That is what we are up against: a natural tendency of the body and mind to move us away from threat and discomfort and *toward* safety and comfort.

Here's how you might unknowingly participate in this pattern of avoidance. When your child begins to express fear that an event will go wrong and that she can't cope with it, your first move is probably to reassure her. "You'll be fine. You'll have fun; just wait and see. You might get a little anxious, but it will pass. If you feel like you just can't spend the night, then you can call me, and I'll come pick you up. But if you stay the whole night, then we'll buy you those skates you've been wanting. How does that sound?"

You will probably get pulled in by your child's expressed fears of catastrophes by questions. Lots of questions. *Am I okay? Is everything safe? Will you show up? What if they laugh? What if I can't fall asleep?*

When each of your reassurances is followed by another fear or doubt, then you get demoralized and frustrated, or perhaps you just want to stop her suffering. So you agree that she just can't handle it and give in to her insistence that she avoid the activity. Then, when the next similar event rolls around, you're both on board: it's too much for her, she can't handle it, she might as well avoid, there's no other choice (see Figure 3.2).

If both you *and* your child can understand this tendency, then we can work together to create a protocol that promotes change. That protocol includes helping your child go *toward* the threat and discomfort. More on that later.

PERFECTLY RIGID

Anxious kids tend to create inflexible standards on two fronts: predictability and perfectionism. And when kids get rigid, worry gets stronger.

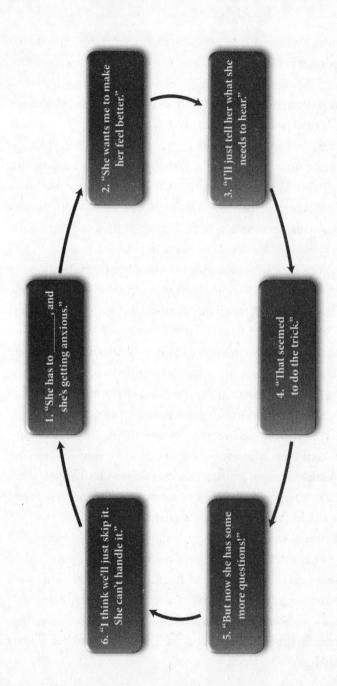

Figure 3.2: How Parents Strengthen Avoidance

As soon as kids require that activities are predictable, they worry that things might change. When they face something new or different—like a substitute teacher at school or a new carpool parent—anxious kids begin to worry, *Hey, this isn't what I'm used to! I'm not sure how this will turn out! And I can't handle that!*

Facing this fear-of-the-new, your child may start firing a barrage of questions or may simply and annoyingly ask the same question repeatedly. *What time will we arrive at the beach? Exactly how many hours does it take to drive there? What time are we leaving? Are you sure?* When kids become unyielding in their demand for an all-knowing crystal ball, the whole family is in trouble.

We also see kids who understand intellectually and rationally that we *can't* know about some changes in advance. We can't know when we'll catch a cold, when our pets will die, or when our computers will crash. They understand that life can be unpredictable, but their worries convince them to try to beat the system by being overly vigilant. Thus, they constantly monitor their bodies for any signs of impending illness, or check on the aging dog all through the night to make sure he's still breathing, or print out each page of a term paper as soon as they type it—all in service of "just to be sure." It's as if they live by the credo that life may be unpredictable for some people, but staying on guard and paying attention gives them an edge over more careless folks. They may not ask questions, but their actions reveal their motto: "Don't leave anything to chance."

We're betting you can predict what we're going to say about perfectionism. Perhaps you've already spent hours trying to convince your fourth-grader that the numbers on the math homework don't have to be printed perfectly, because it's the correct answer that counts most. Maybe you've watched your child repeatedly start drawings and then rip up the paper, over and over, until she dissolves in tears of frustration.

Anxious kids cling to perfectionistic goals. Their rigid view of how activities must unfold makes it painful to learn and to explore, since they believe that perfection counts above all. Making mistakes feels like an intolerable failure, so they either avoid or get stuck compulsively repeating a task until it's just right.

Convincing kids that this is a bad approach is hard. What's wrong with practicing a skill until you master it? Why not make the drawing your best? Checking math homework for errors is a good habit, and sometimes you find errors you missed the first three times.

These traits and behaviors are not all bad. Persistence and high standards lead to success, but an anxious child often does not know when enough is enough. Their drive to be perfect, fueled by a fear of failure, becomes an all-or-nothing strategy that dictates limited outcomes. The perfect drawing? The perfect essay? The perfect outfit? When anxiety is the judge, a child becomes trapped in her own rigid perceptions, unable to see the important role of mistakes and missteps in growing and maturing.

In Chapter 2 we emphasized the value of positive role modeling. You must pay attention to how you handle failure and mistakes. When is something good enough? How do you move on to your next task? What does your family say about screw-ups? The goal is to teach flexibility, which means knowing when to push harder and when to be satisfied with a less-than-perfect result.

Different circumstances require different strategies. When you drive, you are not flexible about stopping at red lights. But when you are doing yard work, you decide when you've picked up enough leaves or weeded adequately. Moviemakers, musicians, chefs, and writers must decide when their masterpieces are done. Do they wonder if it's truly complete, ready to be shared with the world? We're betting such doubt is common, but it's a normal part of the process.

In this chapter's Time to Take Action section we suggest that you explore the world of rigidity and flexibility. We start by asking you to analyze how stressful your family life is, because when any of us are under pressure, we tend to become more anxious and rigid. Introducing some more flexibility into your family routines may plant a seed for your child to grow more tolerant of change.

TIME TO TAKE ACTION:
Applying the Concepts of Chapter 3

Just for Parents

At the start of the chapter we talked about the stressful state of the world. Now is the time to look at your stress and how your schedule might be adding to your child's anxiety. When parents are tightly booked, with deadlines to meet and high expectations for success, children are pulled into these schedules and are often required to participate in a routine that allows little room for error.

What happens when your child makes a mistake, forgets something, or breaks something? How does your stress impact your child's view of flexibility, rigidity, and mistakes? What message do you send to your children?

Take some time and examine the patterns in your family, your lifestyle, and your parenting. The chapters to come provide you and your children the tools to help you shift away from a worried and stressed-out existence. But first, let the following questions help you think about the stress and anxiety in your environment.

• How many structured activities do your children participate in?

- How many nights a week do you eat dinner together as a family?
- If asked, what would your child say about *your* stress and worry?
- How often do you feel pressured by time constraints?
- How often do the adults in the home yell? What time of day is that most likely to happen?
- How often are children punished?
- If free to be totally truthful, what words would your children use to describe your home? What words would you use?

Plant the Seeds . . .
of Flexibility

If anxiety has been running your house, then you have probably generated rigid patterns that have been hanging around, too. When you become rigid—needing to act in a certain way without variation—you end up promoting anxiety by trying to prevent mistakes or limit risk taking. In turn, you may be creating a tense and punitive household.

As we prepare to move into the puzzle pieces, we want you to get your child ready for the rule breaking that's to come. We will ask you and your child to interact in some new ways, like acknowledging out loud how being rigid has sometimes interfered with experiencing new activities. Can you review together any family legends about someone being stubborn and inflexible, even when it didn't make sense? Or someone being flexible and creative in a wonderful way? Any inventors in the family? Innovators?

Now would also be a great time to look at the bibliography of children's books in Appendix C and share some with your child. Many of them tell stories of cognitive flexibility and shifting perspective. For older children, look for movies and novels that support flexibility and imagination—a hero or heroine who acts in a unique way or uses imagination to rectify problems.

Model the Process . . .
of Flexibility

Take a look at the messages you convey to your children about flexibility and rigidity. How are you helping them to distinguish between times when rules are important and when they can be modified? When your routine is disrupted, how do you talk about that in front of your children? Look for opportunities to model flexibility, and talk about how you modified your plans, ideas, or points of view. ("I was planning on making salmon for dinner tonight, but I forgot to defrost it, so let's have pasta instead." "When I first started at this job, I thought Mary was really snobby, but now I know she's just very quiet most of the time.") Also, share stories of times when being flexible and imaginative worked well, talking about situations or events where doing things differently was fun or surprising. ("Aunt Beth gave me a recipe for brownies with avocado, and I thought that sounded gross, but you all just devoured them!")

4

It's Actually *Not* Breaking News

I f you live in fairly wet climates like we do, then you've seen the ads promoting dry basement technology. The goal is to increase living space, keep out moisture, and guarantee that your investment in carpets, furniture, and electronics is protected from spring snow melt or summer floods. These companies eliminate damage by sealing every crack, dehumidifying the air, locking out the wet, and preserving your stuff.

In fact, we modern folks have become rather fond of the concept of elimination—bugs, pests, mold, mildew, germs, dust, weeds, and those unsightly stains on carpets, clothes, and teeth.

You may have tried the elimination approach with worry, too. You did your best to banish uncertainty and discomfort, to keep you and your child out of those situations where worry might show up. You hoped to eliminate worry by simply announcing it doesn't belong or declaring, "There's nothing to worry about." But when your only strategies are to demean, dismiss, or remove anxious worrying, you're going to fail. When you go up against such a mighty challenger, you're going to need cleverer skills.

Why can't you eradicate worry? Because everybody worries and everybody is *supposed* to worry. It's an early-warning signal that we may be moving too quickly without thinking things through, or that we haven't yet completed an important task, or that we are impulsively stepping into a situation for which we are not yet prepared. And, although we hope that it will never happen, worry helps us get ready to escape or fight when facing a true danger.

Anxious kids are going to worry more than others. They may be genetically predisposed to be sensitive to stressors, and they might also pick up the tendency from a parent who is unknowingly teaching them through modeling. Anxious kids may find that their wonderful imaginations have a propensity to exaggerate negative outcomes. If they have adopted a rigid style that seeks perfection and requires predictability, their worries can swell. Moreover, they generally doubt their ability to handle whatever they predict is coming.

Why Kids Worry

- It can serve a useful function (Chapter 1).
  - Helps us slow down when it's smart to take our time
  - Helps us back away from events when it's smart to avoid them
  - Helps us run away or fight when the danger is real
- Genes (Chapter 2)
- Modeling from parents (Chapter 2)
- The stresses of the world (Chapter 3)
- Their imaginations (Chapter 3)
- Being rigid—requiring predictability and perfectionism (Chapter 3)

For all the reasons listed in the box, the goal of eradicating anxious worrying is not only impossible, it's actually likely to backfire. Perhaps you are beginning to see how trying to reassure the anxious child that his fears are exaggerated, or trying to accommodate his requests for comfort and avoidance, only help worry to persist.

In this chapter we're going to leave *eliminate* behind, and move into *expect*. The first piece of the puzzle is EXPECT TO WORRY, and we show you how to shift the way you and your child react to worry by normalizing the arrival of worry and predicting when worry is likely to make an appearance.

Expect
to Worry

Let's go back to basements for a moment. A few hundred years ago, in many parts of the United States the best technology for building houses and their foundations was stone. Strong and permanent and impervious to weather, many of these houses still stand today. As solid as these houses were, the builders back then accepted that eliminating all water from their cellars wasn't possible. So they did something clever—brilliant, even. Go into one of those old stone cellars, and you'll see a small channel around the edges of the cellar floors (often hard-packed earth), not too deep or wide, and sometimes lined with stone. Then, you'll notice the channel leads to a drain that lets the water exit the cellar. Those people obviously said, "We live in a wet place. The water might come in. Let's expect that. And then let's build an exit, so it can flow back out."

We want you and your child to adopt the attitude of Farmer Jones living in Virginia in 1845. What do we mean by this? We know that worry loves the element of surprise, catching its victims off guard. We also know that worry is predictable. Repeat: Worry is *predictable*! It is to your family's advantage to stop being surprised by an experience that is so inevitable.

Any scenario full of "what if" questions—like whether a thunderstorm will ruin the birthday party at the water park—poses a familiar challenge to families: How do you manage an unpredictable or uncertain situation? Here we are talking about the first strategy: expect the arrival of worry's questions when you encounter uncertainty and newness. Of course you're wondering whether the thunderstorm will arrive. Of course you're hoping all goes smoothly, so you're worrying that the party might be cancelled.

THE ARRIVAL OF WORRY

On the final day of the 2012 U.S. Open—one of professional golf's biggest stages—twenty-six-year-old Webb Simpson was six shots behind the lead of Jim Furyk as he stepped up to the tee at the sixth hole. With his characteristic tenacity and magical putting, Simpson bounded forward with four birdies over the next five holes. In his second-ever attempt in a major tournament, Simpson came away with the championship. At the press conference thirty minutes later, Simpson confided, "I've never felt nerves like I did today. A couple of times I had to hit my legs because I couldn't feel them." On his final putt on the eighteenth hole, which would determine if he was going to receive the $1.4 million cash prize, "It got my hands shaking a little," he said, "but I knocked it in."

Many anxious children and adults believe that everybody else handles new and challenging situations free of worry or anxiety. When they see a performer or top athlete like Webb Simpson in action, they assume that person feels comfortable and confident every step of the way. Children who are anxious on the first day of school or who are tearful when they head off to camp believe that their peers are happily saying good-bye without a moment's hesitation.

The truth is that even those who are highly skilled and successful at what they do feel worry and doubt along the way. Authors with numerous published books sit down to start a new one and wonder if they have anything else worthwhile to say. People who travel regularly might still feel anxious and check their flight status when the weather report looks problematic. Kids who excitedly pack for camp can still feel a wave of uncertainty as their parents pull away from camp and head home.

How to Make Worry Bigger

We tend to worry when . . .	But we *really* worry when . . .
We're trying something new or different.	*We need it to go exactly right.*
We're unsure about our plans.	*We need to be sure.*
We have a lot of "what if" questions.	*We need to answer all of them.*
We have to perform.	*We don't feel prepared, or we are afraid we'll be criticized or fail.*

When we understand that such thoughts and feelings are a normal part of the process, we can give ourselves permission to move forward. We don't have to interpret such feelings as a signal to stop.

In the last chapter, we talked about anxious kids creating high standards on two fronts: demanding to know that activities will turn out exactly as they need them and insisting that tasks be performed perfectly. When they hold those expectations, then worry becomes more intrusive. That's how it is for all of us: the more we create rigid criteria for success, the more we struggle with activities.

Increased worry goes hand-in-hand with our insistence that the uncertain world abide by our rigid expectations. Consider what it's like when you are trying a new or different activity: pitching a novel idea to your boss, trying snowboarding for the first time, or inviting guests to a new restaurant. You can expect some worries to pop up, of course. But as soon as you decide that this new activity must go exactly your way, the pressure and tension expand and overwhelm. Your boss has to love the idea. You must quickly learn your new center of gravity on the board. The restaurant must be quiet enough, your guests must love the food, and the conversation must flow smoothly. When you insist on outcome when that result is not guaranteed, then worry won't just show up, it will begin to dominate.

If all activities must unfold according to the plans we outline, or if all our questions must be answered before we venture out, then either we spend more of our mental time worrying or we back away from those activities. If failure is unacceptable, or if any criticism by another cannot be tolerated, then we obsess about and overprepare for our performance. If that worry and preparation feel too shaky to guarantee our expected outcome, then we back away from the activity.

Imagine getting a significant promotion at work. You're excited because it's a great opportunity with a salary increase, but you feel anxious about the new level of responsibility, how your coworkers will respond to you, and whether your hours will increase too much.

The Times When Kids Might Worry

Trying something new	*First day of school, substitute teacher, jumping off diving board, a new bus driver, starting karate lessons, the first airplane flight*
Unsure about plans	*Will we be allowed to have a sleepover? Will the rain cancel our party? Will Mom's work schedule change?*
Lots of "what if" questions	*Will I get sick on our trip? Will I forget my homework? Will my dog die? What if the movie is scary and loud? What if I need to go to the bathroom while I'm on the school bus? Will I like the trip? What will happen?*
Performance	*Getting called on in class, running in cross-country meet, reciting poem in class, sparring in karate*
Something scary is happening	*Thunderstorms, surgery, driving in a snowstorm, being chased by a dog, climbing too high in a tree, hearing parents yelling*

You have two possible approaches. Option one is that you can tell yourself that if you feel too anxious on the first day, it means this job is too much for you. You can rely on your gut to guide you, and if you're not feeling right about it, you can conclude it's not a good fit. If you can't sleep the night before your first day, you see this as a predictor of not-so-good things to come.

Option two is reminding yourself that feeling anxious on the first day (or week or month) of a new position is normal, because you're learning new skills, you want to do well, and you don't yet know exactly how you'll navigate through these new challenges. You expect to feel anxious, telling yourself that you can be excited and nervous at the same time. You don't have much of an appetite for breakfast, so you pack a snack for later when your hunger shows up again. You decide to have only one cup of coffee instead of two this first day, as your normal first-day jitters will be stimulating enough.

Many anxious families treat the normal arrival of worry as breaking news, even if it has happened repeatedly in the past. When children begin to show signs of anxiety about a new activity, parents often escalate right along with them, surprised and frustrated that it's happening (again).

Stop acting startled by each new occurrence of worry and help your child do the same. Your job as a parent is to model how common and expected these feelings can be. The goal of this puzzle piece is to change the initial reaction that your child has to uneasy feelings and to change yours as well. Worry is contagious.

A Tale of Two Teeth Cleanings

If your child has a hard time separating, help her expect worry to show up, as it does for lots of kids when they say good-bye and head off to a new activity. If you reframe those uncomfortable butterflies and tummy aches that arrive at the end of summer as "first-day-of-school feelings" and welcome them as a routine part of starting a new school year, you are teaching the skill of allowing uncertainty and discomfort to be a part of the experience, not an emergency.

Here are two examples of conversations between a parent and a child worried about a visit to the dentist. The first conversation illustrates being surprised by worry, and then trying to eliminate it. (*Hint:* The second conversation is the better one.)

GINA: I don't want to go to the dentist! I don't like it. It's going to hurt. Please don't make me go!

MOM: Now, that's silly, Gina! Why are you getting worried about this? You've been to the dentist every year since you were four. There's nothing to worry about. Dr. Albee is a very nice dentist, and it's just a cleaning.

GINA: I *always* hate it, every single time we go. What if I have a cavity? What if he says I'm not brushing enough?

MOM: Oh, for goodness sake! Stop worrying. You're making this into a big problem for nothing.

GINA: I'm going to freak out if you take me. I won't get out of the car!

MOM: I'm surprised you're acting this way.

Expect to Worry

- It's normal, it's common, and it can be helpful.

In this second conversation, assume that Mom and Gina have been learning together about how worry has been dominating their lives, and they've been working on developing a new approach. Listen to how they respond differently to the arrival of worry. Mom even models how normal it is to feel anxious before a doctor's visit.

GINA: I hate going to the dentist! Why do I have to go? I feel sick.

MOM: I know you don't like it. Sounds like your worry has shown up again, like it usually does when you have to go to the dentist. I felt the same way when I had to go to my doctor's appointment last month.

GINA: Well, I'm not going, and you can't make me. Why are you making me?

MOM: You and I both know why you go to the dentist, and we also know why your worry is showing up. Good old predictable worry . . . doesn't know exactly what's going to happen at the dentist today, so thinks you should skip it completely. I'm not surprised, are you?

GINA: I guess not. Worry does this a lot.

MOM: Well, tell worry to get into the car. We'll talk to him on the way to Dr. Albee's office.

This dialogue illustrates an essential shift you must make in your perspective about worry: it's normal, it's common, and it's a part of growing and living. Your child needs to learn to recognize it and handle it. As we've talked about it, worry can sometimes serve a valuable purpose, but it *always* thinks it's being helpful, even when it's not. By learning more about how worry operates, you can coach your child on when to ignore those normal and expected worried thoughts— and move on with life—and when to pay attention to them.

The dialogue also hints at where we go next. Once you and your child become more accepting of worry and less surprised by it, you can learn to respond consistently to new and uncertain situations without your stress level rising. Rather than anxiously anticipating when the worry will show up, dreading the battles it will create, and attempting to avoid the conflict altogether, you set a different tone and then stand your ground. You see anxiety as something to be addressed—and in Chapter 5 we teach how anyone in your family can talk to it.

Now you have the first of our seven pieces of the puzzle of childhood anxiety. In the upcoming chapters we introduce five more pieces and advise you on the most important changes needed to strengthen your family. Once you get to Chapter 11, you will learn how to help your child study these same puzzle pieces. Then in Chapter 12 you'll be ready for the final puzzle piece: TAKE ACTION ON YOUR PLAN. That's when you will work as a team to apply these strategies to your child's specific anxious reactions.

As you already know, there is no magic trick that parents can use to convince a fearful child to push through fears by acting courageously. No simple message persuades an anxious child to act more independently. Consider the suggestions that we offer in the following "Time to Take Action" section as the recommended ways to prepare your family for the hard work ahead. Trust that if you apply these suggestions now, your entire family will be better prepared for the work that comes in Chapters 11 and 12.

TIME TO TAKE ACTION:
Applying the Concepts of Chapter 4

Plant the Seeds . . . of Normalizing Worry
and Expecting Worry to Show Up

1. Because worry has likely caused a fair amount of chaos in your family, you and other family members might be responding to its arrival with some intense emotions. Begin the shift to normalizing worry by talking in the presence of your child about the routine times when worry shows up for you. The goal is to demonstrate to your child that it's part of the process when you are handling new situations, when you have a performance, or when something is important to you. Talk at the dinner table about how worry showed up during the day and how you expected it to do so in that situation. ("I met that new client I told you about, and of course I felt pretty nervous. I think he probably felt my sweaty palms when we shook hands.")

2. Look for opportunities to point out when someone is successful at doing something, but also acknowledges nervousness during the process. Athletes, performers, contestants, new teachers . . . they often make statements about working through their jitters at the start of an important event. ("Ringo Starr was on TV talking about his stage fright when he was in the Beatles. He felt really anxious before every performance, but he said once he started playing his drums, he was okay. He just accepted it was going to happen that way.")

3. Plant the seeds that being surprised by something normal and expected doesn't make much sense. People who live in Florida

being surprised by heat in the summer? Mothers buying white couches and being surprised when the kids make the cushions dirty? Leaving cupcakes on the kitchen counter and being surprised to find that your very big dog stood up on his back legs and ate them when you went to bed?

Model the Process . . .
of *Not* Being Surprised When Worry Shows Up

How do you manage your feelings when you start a project that requires a new skill set or when you have to perform in front of others? How do you handle the worried thoughts that show up when things are uncertain? As your child detects your reactions, including your worry, she begins to assimilate your style. Can you acknowledge when you're nervous about something? What do you say? How do you behave? How do you show your child that worry is normal, or how do you model being surprised? Pay attention to your words and actions, and then ask yourself, *Am I giving the message that I* shouldn't worry *in this situation?* For example, notice the difference between "I'm going to leave a few minutes early for the office this morning because I have to present something important, and I like some extra time when I'm nervous" and "I'm so nervous about this meeting. Why do I always feel this way? I'm going to leave early because I'm freaking out." And what messages are you giving when you say *nothing* about your distress on those mornings, but you rush around, look and feel distant and uptight, and snap at your partner or one of your kids?

5

Same Old Worry,
Very Different Responses

I n the last chapter we taught you and your child to expect worry to
show up. Even without picking up this book, Lucille, the mother
of a very anxious ten-year-old son, already embraces this concept—
sort of. Here's what she said during her first office visit:

***

Toby is anxious, and we know that's how he'll be. My
grandmother and her sister were very anxious people. I had
a terrible time getting through school and talking to people.
I sometimes wonder how I managed to meet my husband!
No one was surprised when Toby started refusing to leave
my side. He sleeps on a mattress in our room every night.
That helps us all feel better. With my family history, it's just a
given he's going to be plagued by this thing. It's in our genes.
It's who we are. I jokingly tell my husband to start fixing up
the basement now, because that's where Toby will be living!

***

Lucille does a great job of expecting worry to show up, even seeing it as normal in her own anxious family. However, in her efforts to
help, Lucille makes the common mistake of seeing Toby's avoidant
and fearful behavior as an inevitable, permanent part of his life. She
doesn't want him to be anxious—she knows what a daily struggle it
can be—but she conveys to Toby (and probably to teachers, friends,
and family members) that this is who he is in a global and fixed way.

Why is this a problem? Because as we move forward into the next
six puzzle pieces, we are going to ask you and your child to take unfamiliar action and to experience discomfort. When you expect worry
to show up and then accept its dominant presence, you stop there.
You say to the worry, "Well, I knew you'd show up; there's nothing
I can do about that. I acknowledge that you're in charge, so I'll play
by your rules now." We know that worry is exhausting, but changing
this pattern requires courage and energy. Though we expect anxiety
to be a part of life, *we do not accept, and neither should you,* that anxiety must permanently rule your family and your child.

Give your child the message that worry is a normal part of growing and learning, a necessary part of life experience, but emphasize
that anxiety is only a part of your child's whole self. Moving away
from this broad definition of your child or your family as "anxious"
is going to be essential as you learn to use the next puzzle piece: TALK
TO YOUR WORRY.

This puzzle piece addresses the common problem of listening
to what worry has to say and believing it without question. Most
anxious people experience the majority of their worried thoughts
as helpful and protective—and sometimes they are—but being able
to recognize the difference between helpful information and the
dominating, unhelpful chatter of anxiety requires a different tactic:
externalization.

Talk to
Your Worry

Externalization puts anxious worry outside of you, allowing you to see the worry and its messages from a different perspective. With the help of a little distance, worriers can hear and see how anxiety operates without immediately accepting the validity of its fears and demands. This concept is often new to adults and children alike, an option they never considered. *Don't listen to my anxiety? Ignore those kinds of thoughts?* Absolutely! Worry will show up to promote avoidance again and again, but you and your child don't need to buy into its rigid point of view.

Externalize the Anxious Worries

- Personify worry as an object outside of yourself.
  Attribute purpose and motivation to it. Perceive yourself as in a relationship with your anxieties. Learn to hear and talk to your worry.

Do you have anyone in your life who has an opinion about everything? Someone who offers advice whether you want it or not—a colleague, family member, or neighbor who consistently corrects you? How do you manage this person? Do you take all the advice, follow every suggestion, buy every recommended product, go to every specialist, eat at every restaurant, see every movie, and eliminate every food group? You get the point. There comes a time when you nod and smile politely while thinking about what you need at the grocery store, or you silently thank the inventor of caller ID and don't pick up the phone when he or she calls.

Like with the annoying know-it-all, you have to stop letting anxiety distract you from handling the real issues. Anxiety is not that creative once you step back and see how it operates. Even though it may throw a variety of specific problems at your family, its primary messages remain fairly consistent. The same anxiety-provoking thoughts show up again and again. You and your child don't have to remain at the mercy of the voice of worry!

Rather than being pulled into the catastrophic visions that your anxiety generates, your child can learn to move away from it and take back some control. At the end of this chapter, we suggest ways that she can employ her powerful imagination to personify her anxious worrying, to conceive of it as outside of herself, and even give it a name.

You can help the process by describing your own tendency to worry and talking to your child about it. You can even give *your* anxious worries a kid-friendly name. However, remember that modeling any of these strategies does not mean sharing adult-only worries with your child.

WHO'S THE BOSS?

We're not asking kids to learn to address worry in such a way that they get rid of it. That's not going to happen. Keep in mind that worry thinks it's taking care of us, so it's going to keep intruding into our thoughts about trying new activities. But we do want children to learn how to *talk* to their worries, showing worry, and themselves, that they can handle it. Anxious worrying is not allowed to be the boss. Finding a voice to talk to worry is the beginning of learning how to manage it.

Sharing Worries with Your Child

- *Good Modeling*: "My worry wart kept bugging me about being late for my dentist appointment!"
- *Bad Modeling*: "My worry wart kept asking me if Grandma was going to survive her heart surgery!" (Sharing an adult-only worry)

Children can choose three broad ways to talk to their anxious worry: assume worry will show up this time (expect it), offer reassurance to that insecure part of them (take care of it), or, if they're annoyed by bothersome worry, tell it to get lost (boss it around).

Expect it. Remember from Chapter 4 that worry shows up on a regular basis for all of us. The four most common times? When we're trying a new activity, when we're not sure about our plans and we need to tie them down, when we have a lot of "what if" questions regarding events going wrong, and when we have to perform. Treating our worries like a surprise, day after day, just makes the thoughts more powerful. As kids begin to understand their worries, they can see that it is only trying to protect them. So their messages to it can simply imply that hearing it is no big deal: *Oh, there you are. You usually show up about this time.* Some kids even invite the worry along on their adventure because it helps them stay safe. If they're skateboarding home from school, worry can remind them to watch out for those big cracks in the sidewalk.

Take care of it. Other children recognize their worried thoughts as coming from a scared side of them that thinks they are being threatened by something that they can't handle. Their goal is to reassure the worrier within them. They talk to it gently, and they intend to take over for the scared and avoidant side. Their communication may sound like, *It's okay. I can handle whatever happens.*

Boss it around. Sometimes kids are not intimidated by their worries but rather are annoyed and frustrated. Anxiety has caused them to miss out on activities they enjoy. They aren't going to listen to it anymore, and they want it gone. These kids can talk tough to their worry and may use strong language to push it back. If you're like most parents, you'll probably feel delighted if your child starts saying to worry, "*Knock it off!* Stop trying to scare me!" When children get to this stage, they may ask you for special permission to use words that are normally off limits at home, like "stupid" or "jerk." Use your judgment and family rules on this one. Sometimes by allowing them to use such a disrespectful word *only* for their anxious worries, you can help them relate to these worries in a powerful and fun kind of way. However, we don't suggest allowing children to cross the line with language that is truly inappropriate, like swearing.

Different Ways Kids Can Talk to Worry

Expect It	Take Care of It	Boss It Around
"I know you're just trying to help." "You usually show up at these times, so I'm not surprised by you." "Worry is a part of learning something new. I'm supposed to feel this way."	"I'm going to feel nervous, and then it'll be over." "It's okay; things will work out." "It's okay. I can handle whatever happens." "I'm safe, even though I feel scared."	"I'll get back to you on that, worry." "You're not helping. I'm going to ignore you." "I know you're there, but I'm busy." "Knock it off! Stop trying to scare me!" "You're ruining my fun. I've had it with you."

We have emphasized throughout the early chapters that worry is not always a problem, and listening to worry sometimes slows kids down in helpful ways as they solve problems. We've had children decide to create two worry parts within themselves: the one that knows how to slow down and be wise, and the one that always wants to avoid activities and to freak out, no matter what. One girl called them her "Sensible Worry" and her "Bossy Worry," and she learned to distinguish between the two. *Who should I listen to, and who should I ignore?* became a question she asked herself—a helpful skill as she moved into adolescence.

Teaching your child this skill of differentiation—namely, the ability to know when to listen and when to ignore—can take some practice, and as a parent you can promote this skill development in lots of different areas. Children should consider the following types of questions: *How do I determine if a dog is safe to pet or is better avoided? How do I decide if I should respond to an adult who says hello to me if I don't know her? When do I try a new and different food, and when do I say, "No thanks"? Am I so sick that I need to stay home from school, or can I make it through the day? Is it safe enough to swim in the ocean today, or are the waves too rough?*

Anxious children and anxious parents usually err on the side of caution, perhaps with global rules that prevent any experimenting. "Never go near a dog you don't know." "I don't eat any vegetables, and I won't try them either." "I'll never get my driver's license because driving is dangerous." We are recommending flexible thinking rather than global avoidance. You'll have a chance to practice this with your child in the exercises at the end of the chapter.

Externalizing the worry and being able to recognize its repetitive tactics help you and your child create some distance from it. Once you can see it as separate and have a strategy to talk to it, your perspective and reactions begin to change. Easy, right? Not always. As you work together to recognize, externalize, and then talk to worry, we want you to be prepared for some of the tactics worry uses to regain its powerful status and how to respond when such tactics show up.

THEY TALK MORE, YOU TALK LESS

Back in Chapter 2 we described the most common patterns that parents fall into when dealing with anxiety in their families. These tendencies usually involve the parents doing *more* to make the anxious child feel better: more explaining, more reassuring, more accommodation, and more comforting. As we move through the puzzle pieces, you should switch out of the role of explainer and fixer and into the role of supporter and coach. Your child needs to take charge, and he can start by learning how to talk to worry. Your child must find his own voice, and you must use yours less.

Worry engages two clever tactics to pull parents into "explainer and fixer" mode: reassurance seeking and the content trap. If you're tired of constantly talking in circles to your child about worry, then recognizing and changing these two patterns can help. We'll guide you on how to respond differently.

Worry's Tactics to Get Parents Overinvolved

- **Reassurance seeking:** Kids ask repetitive questions regarding certainty and comfort.
- **The content trap:** The family focuses on the specific event versus addressing the common pattern across events.

Let's start with reassurance seeking. Worried children may persistently ask for certainty and comfort as they approach new situations or challenges. The parents of such kids are quite familiar with this pattern. Worried thoughts gain power inside a child's mind because they become repetitive and go unchallenged. Children become victims of unchecked messages such as, *I can't let anyone be upset with me, I have to know exactly how this will turn out, I can't handle fourth grade, I can't make* any *mistakes,* or *What if I screw up?* They wall themselves off in their own private compound of rigidly high standards, untouched by past successes or supportive logic, fearfully absorbed by their repeated thoughts. Once they reach this state, worried children choose one of two paths to quiet the noise. Either they completely back away from the activity or they seek security from someone else. Together, your family must interrupt this pattern.

When worried children attempt to feel less anxious by seeking reassurance from their parents, they are looking for confidence and guarantees. They want us to tell them that whatever they fear (making a mistake, vomiting, having a bad dream) will never happen, or it won't happen today, or it won't be so bad. Parents find themselves offering almost constant words of support and comfort. They remind their child of how specific activities have gone fine in the past, provide statistics about improbabilities, and present concise lectures about the irrationality of that specific fear.

But the relief is fleeting at best. You probably know what it's like to try to talk your worried child out of her erroneous beliefs—or to offer reassurance over and over, only to have your words drift away like mist.

Take Evelyn, who worried constantly that her mother, Tracy, would accidentally leave her somewhere—at school, in the grocery store, at the library. Tracy had never actually forgotten Evelyn anywhere, and she was now especially vigilant about arriving on time. Her frustration with Evelyn's persistent questioning was growing. "Are you going to be at school on time?" "Will you stay near me in the store?" "You're not going to leave without me, are you?" Tracy answered the questions over and over, repeatedly reminding Evelyn that she had never abandoned her in the past. Occasionally she attempted to talk about what *would* happen if they got separated, about how they could solve that problem. But that discussion immediately caused Evelyn to express even more clingy and insecure behavior.

We understand how intuitive it feels to offer your child comfort and reassurance. We also know the importance, even to adults, of external, loving guidance. We're not talking about dropping a six-year-old at the bus stop on the first day of kindergarten so that she'll learn to cope, or even sending a sixteen-year-old off to his driver's test without a good-luck hug and a little pep talk. We're talking about coaching worried kids such as Evelyn to recognize worry and externalize it as a way to step out of its powerful grip.

Offering reassurance is an easy trap to fall into. Worried kids fail to recall what they've accomplished. They don't remind themselves of previous obstacles overcome, and they don't realize that being nervous is normal in many situations. They never think, *I can handle this because I've done it before,* or *Of course I feel nervous on the first day of school.* They don't have a voice to talk to the worry, and instead they look to trusted adults to step in and manage their thoughts and feelings.

If they are forced into action, they depend on others to offer all the reminders, over and over. When Evelyn bombarded Tracy with questions about being left, Tracy answered almost automatically just to keep their schedule running smoothly. In the short-term it was quicker and more efficient for Mom to reassure. Twenty repetitive responses of "Yes, I'll be there" and "You won't get lost" seemed to work better than one long and often fruitless discussion about Mom's reliability or Evelyn's option to use a cell phone if needed. Keeping Evelyn comfortable and certain worked, as long as Tracy was around and willing to play by worry's rules. Evelyn depended on her mother's words but had no words of her own.

Here's what we want you to do instead: Cue your child to externalize worry and talk to it. When your child asks for reassurance, you can remind him to give *himself* the reassurance he wants. Rather than answering the question outright, you can ask, "How might *you* answer that?" or "That sounds like worry talking. What can you say back?" We give you a number of possible responses as the chapter continues.

Coaching Your Child Without Reassuring the Worry

- Remain consistent and calm.

- Acknowledge worry's presence and how uncomfortable your child feels.

- Be clear that you are no longer going to give worry what it wants or fall for its tricks.

- Remind your child to externalize worry and talk back to it:

  ◆ "How might you answer that?"

  ◆ "That sounds like worry talking. What can you say back?"

  ◆ "Why don't you try telling me? I'll give you some clues if you get stuck."

This is a process, and your child needs to learn the skill. You might say, "I've answered that before, and we've been through this same situation many times. Instead of me telling you, how about *you* tell you? I'll give you some clues if you get stuck." The goal is to get your child to step away from the worry, talk to it, and do the internal work that leads to independent problem solving.

The exercises at the end of the chapter give you specific ways to help your child develop this puzzle piece of separating from anxious worry and then learning to talk to it. After practicing the skill for a while, children often come up with a few favorite set responses when worry starts to show up.

Beware the Content Trap

Offering reassurance also pulls you into the *content versus process trap*. Here's what we mean: When you reassure your child about the specific thing that makes him anxious, you are failing to address the bigger-picture work necessary to overcome this problem. That's what kept Tracy and her daughter stuck: they stayed focused on the topic of Mom forgetting Evelyn. You can never learn how to beat worry if the two of you keep talking about event after event instead of addressing the pattern that traps you.

Look at how your responses might keep worry strong, and experiment with ways to change your pattern. Remember, our goal is to teach the skills necessary to handle all sorts of worry, not to focus on remedying worry about a single event. The problem is not whether kids at school like your child, or if the teacher will be disappointed in her for a punctuation error. You may spend lots of time lessening your child's worry about bee stings when she's six, only to find yourself in the same type of discussion when she's worrying about getting her driver's license at sixteen. The content changes. Your task is to attend to the *process* of worry so that your child knows how to respond to new content areas that inevitably arise as she grows older.

Most parents do get caught up in the content trap. Even after they learn about it, they find themselves answering content questions or giving information that temporarily relieves the worry. Solving a problem through reassurance is just another form of avoidance—a short-term fix that deals with a specific current problem but doesn't teach a skill your child can use to handle his *pattern* of worrying. If you and your child understand how worry works across a variety of contexts and how to talk to it, you're both better equipped to handle whatever comes up as you move through each new stage of childhood development.

Here are some examples of reassurance, the content trap, and the more positive approach of cueing for externalization.

Event	Offering Reassurance	Content Trap	Cueing Externalization
Every morning, child worries about vomiting at school.	*"You won't vomit at school today. You look fine to me. You're not sick."*	*"If you feel sick, go to the nurse. She'll help you. It's not a big deal to vomit. Why do you think you're going to vomit every day?"*	*"That sounds like worry talking. What would you like to say back?"*
Child is scared to sleep in own room.	*"Your room is fine. There's nothing in here. If you need me, just call, but you're okay."*	*"We already looked under the bed, and there are no monsters. Daddy put a very strong lock on the door last week, so we're safe here."*	*"Your worry says that every night. What do you need to tell that bossy worry?"*
Child texts Mom all day to find out where she is.	*"I'm at work, as always. I'll be there to get you after your practice at 4:30. I'll let you know if I go somewhere else."*	*"You don't need to keep texting me. Stop worrying about where I am. We've talked about my schedule."*	*"When your worry texts me, I'm not going to respond to it. Before you send a text, check and make sure it's not worry in charge."*
Teen worries if she has said or will say the right things in social situations.	*"I'm sure you did fine! When I hear you with friends, you do just great."*	*"Tell me what you said, and I can see if it's awkward or not."*	*"I can hear how worry makes you doubt yourself in many situations. Can you hear it talking to you, too?"*

Pushing Back

When you start changing your responses to worry, get ready for a bit—actually, a lot—of resistance. You're changing the rules, and rigid worry finds this unacceptable. So ease in. When you start to discuss this strategy of talking to worry, work with your child and come up with phrases to use while you practice. Keep in mind that the content is not the focus here, but how your child responds to worry when it shows up. Responses to worry can fall into the few categories we talked about: expect to worry, take care of worry, or boss worry around. Let's take being afraid of tunnels as an example.

Let's pretend we're getting close to that tunnel on the way to Aunt Josie's house. Worry shows up, but we're prepared! What can we say? Let's expect it first:

Oh, hi, worry. Yes, there's a tunnel ahead, so we knew you'd show up. What a surprise . . . *not!* Worry likes to show up when we get close to the tunnel.

Now let's take care of it:

Okay, worry, you can hide under the seat, and I'll get us through. Easy there, worry, we can handle this. Worry, we knew this was coming. We're scared, but we're okay.

Or how about a bit of bossiness?

Really, worry? You are not going to get me going! How many times are you going to talk to me about this tunnel? You think I can't handle it, but you give me bad advice. Worry, I'm so done with you! Knock it off!

Sometimes younger children have fun choosing an absurd topic. It makes them laugh and helps them understand and hear that this is truly *not about content*. Make up a silly worry, like being afraid of pancakes or rainbows, or worrying that a pig will move into the living room. For teens, allow them to pick something ridiculous, a worry that makes you roll your eyes. Everyone can discover together that the words remain virtually the same, whether the topic is silly or serious, real or ridiculous. This activity offers a good way to rehearse so that the process is familiar when the worry feels more intense.

Practice helps, of course, but when your child's anxiety shows up for real, your suggestions that she talk to it may well be met with anger and denial. When you consistently say, "To me, that sounds like worry talking," your child will likely respond with, "It's not my worry! It's me! I don't want to go to the party. Stop telling me it's worry!" Your job is to remain consistent and calm. Acknowledge worry's presence and how uncomfortable it makes your child feel, but be clear that you are no longer going to give worry what it wants or fall for its tricks.

Remember that talking back to worry does not mean pretending it doesn't exist or that it doesn't make your child feel scared, shaky, or sick. The worry is real, and the physical reactions are real. You are sending the message that worry has been, up until now, powerful and controlling, but you and your child are no longer willing to let it call the shots. *Recognize anxiety, don't deny it. Hear worry, but don't obey it.*

Here's how one mom described handling her child's anger when she began cueing him to talk back to worry:

***

My son Bobby was sure he was going to throw up on the school bus. Every morning, he would start telling me how he felt sick, and how he was sure he'd throw up if I made him ride the bus. We started using the strategies and came up with how he would talk to the worry when it showed up. Bobby was enthusiastic when we practiced, but in the morning when his worry showed up, he refused to buy into the plan. He told me it was *not* his worry. He really was feeling sick and told me I was a horrible mother for not believing him. He knew what worry felt like, and this was *real* sickness, not worry. When I told him to talk back to the worry, he refused because *this wasn't worry!* I stayed calm (on the outside) and said, "Bobby, I know you feel scared and sick, but I'm tired of worry bossing you around like this." Then I told him I would talk back to worry myself. I put my arm around his shoulders and started wagging my finger at worry, saying, "Hey! Mr. Worry! I'm not falling for it this time. My son Bobby has been listening to you for too long, and you've been running my life, too. I know you won't give up easily, but neither will we." We had to work on things for a while, but Bobby felt like I was on his side and I wasn't ignoring how powerful the worry felt to him, so he didn't have to argue with me and convince me anymore.

***

As you begin this process, your child will be confronted with her anxiety and your shifting reactions. She won't understand why you're refusing to do what feels easier in the moment. She will want you to provide reassurance like you've always done. She might beg you to just answer the question so that you can both move on. Wouldn't that be smoother and quicker?

From her perspective, she believes her strategies of listening to worry have been working fine, especially compared to what you're asking of her now. So don't simply impose this change. Make sure that you are laying the groundwork to help your child understand how worry works and why it needs to go. When you and your child recognize how much anxiety has been controlling both of you, you'll be more willing to experiment with these uncomfortable changes—and being willing to be uncomfortable is exactly where we're headed in the next two chapters.

These next suggestions reinforce the skills you have been reading about and can help you and your child start shifting your perspectives and reactions. We're moving fully into the heart of the puzzle pieces now, so our job—and yours—is to keep the momentum and the action going.

TIME TO TAKE ACTION:
Applying the Concepts of Chapter 5

Just for Parents

Your job is to model this technique of externalization in your own life. Before moving to the next chapter, take a few moments to reflect upon the following:

- How do you respond to worry, either your own or your child's, when it shows up? Are you listening to worry?
- What do you say to others who might define you or your child as anxious? Do you speak as though you believe worry to be *global* or *permanent*? Or do you see and treat it as only one *part* of you?
- Pay attention to what we call "safety chatter." How often do you talk to your child in the voice of worry? Ask a friend, partner, or spouse to point out when you talk like worry. (They should do this privately, instead of in front of your child.)

Plant the Seeds . . .
of Externalizing and Talking Back to Worry

Make a habit of pointing out to your child when you observe people (an athlete, a celebrity, a neighbor, etc.) allowing worry to control them. Better yet, note when someone talks to the worry and then succeeds at an activity. People often say, "I think my nerves got the best of me," or "Even though I was scared, I put it aside and got through it." Talk to your child about how that person did—or didn't—externalize their worries, based on what action they took and what they said about their worries.

Model the Process . . .
of Externalizing Worry

1. Show your child how to talk to worry, and even to talk back to it, by doing it yourself. Throw in statements like, "Boy, my worry was talking up a storm while I was working on that project! It distracted me at first, but then I told worry to leave me alone."

2. Model externalization with other emotional states as well. Be aware of the bigger goal of emotional management, the ability to step away from your feelings when necessary, so that you can handle the challenge in front of you. Externalize frustration, anger, even silliness. "I was so mad when my computer crashed that I imagined throwing it out the window, but I threw the frustration out the window instead and figured out what I had to do next," or "When I was at church, I started thinking about that funny show we were watching last night, and I had to put my silliness away so that I wouldn't start giggling out loud!"

The More Unsure, the Better

A story from Lynn ...

***

As I prepared for my next appointment—session three with Janet and ten-year-old Christie—I looked over my notes from the last session. I was anticipating a report from the mother-daughter team on their progress toward a more independent bedtime routine. Every night for as long as the family could remember, Janet read to Christie until she fell asleep. Although they reported this as an enjoyable ritual that they both valued, in reality it was often limiting and inconvenient. Christie would stay awake until 9:30 or 10:00 PM and refuse to let her mother leave her room until she was "totally out." Janet didn't go out with friends or her husband, David, in the evening because Christie didn't trust her father or the babysitter to follow the protocol. Janet was exhausted at the end of her day, but had no time for herself or David. Several times a week she ended up falling asleep in Christie's bed while reading, only to awake in the middle of the night and quietly find her way back to her own bed. No one was getting the sleep needed.

As I stepped into the waiting room, I was a bit surprised to see Janet waiting for me, but no Christie. "I have to talk about the plan," she said. "I'm having trouble following through." The game plan involved Christie externalizing and talking back to her worry and Janet leaving the bedroom after they read a chapter together.

She then described what was happening at night. Christie begged her mom to stay longer in the bedroom or to put off the new plan until the weekend. She whined, cried, and at times became angry and threatening. She even told Janet that she might do "something drastic," like run away from home or scream at the top of her lungs until the neighbors called the police.

Janet's face expressed a combination of fear, sadness, and fatigue. "Last night, Christie yelled at me, 'You keep telling me that nothing will happen if you leave, but what if something does happen? What if you're wrong and I die in my sleep? Or the house catches on fire? Would you be able to live with that? Would you?'"

✳✳✳

Back in Chapter 2, we talked about the common patterns that anxious families fall into, and Janet and Christie were engaged in most of them. Janet, with a history of anxiety and worry herself, tried to keep Christie safe and comfortable. She didn't want her daughter to suffer like she had, and staying in the bedroom was as close as she could come to guaranteeing that Christie would remain calm. Janet constantly reassured Christie that she was safe, although it was never enough. Any variation from the expected routine could set off a tantrum of screaming and aggressive threats. Anxiety was running the show in this family.

Common Patterns in Anxious Families

- Rescuing, reassuring, and overprotecting; providing certainty
- Identifying a child as a worrier because it "runs in the family"
- Stuck in the content trap
- Allowing bad behaviors because of "the anxiety"
- Modeling with your own anxious behavior
- Pushing too hard; becoming angry and explosive

Janet—like virtually every parent we meet—was also stuck in the content trap, caught up in the particulars of each worry, trying to give comfort through reassurance, and accommodating each new fear. Afraid of the dark? Parents buy a nightlight or stay in the room each night. Doesn't trust babysitters? Parents don't go anywhere. On and on. Each new fear leads to another reassurance and another accommodation.

By now you understand why this gets parents nowhere fast. When you put your effort toward trying to fix the details of each worry, anxiety gets quiet, but only for a short time.

* * *

As Janet and I talked about her struggle with the failed plan, she began to sense how her need for certainty was as powerful as Christie's. "I keep thinking, *What if something does happen during the night? Isn't staying in Christie's bed with her a small price to pay if it prevents the unthinkable from happening?*"

I reminded Janet of our first session, when her husband, David, was there, too. "The two of them are a team," he told us. "I'm not so sure that Janet wants to leave Christie alone in her bed. She knows she *should*, but she's always been afraid of something happening to her baby." In this third session she started to realize that David was right: she wasn't willing to feel uncertain and take any kind of risk. And Christie was right, too: Janet couldn't tolerate even thinking about the possibility that something could go wrong, even something improbable or irrational.

* * *

Given her fears and her attachment to her mom, we could give Christie a diagnosis of one of the anxiety disorders. You or your child may already have such a diagnosis, such as generalized anxiety disorder, separation anxiety, or a phobia. This information can sometimes be helpful, but you've probably already noticed that we don't have chapters on each of the different diagnoses. Our approach focuses much more on what the anxiety disorders have in common—what anxiety does repeatedly in all sorts of situations—because learning how to respond to the similarities, rather than the differences, offers a more versatile and effective strategy to handle anxiety now and

throughout your family's life cycle. We are not going small, present-
ing you with the details of specific anxieties. We want you to see the
big picture.

This chapter and the one that follows introduce you to this big-
picture approach, and it's the core of what Janet, Christie, and your
family need to embrace in order to truly beat anxiety and worry. All
families need a devoted willingness to be uncertain and uncomfortable, and to tolerate risk.

People invent lots of homemade strategies that help them deal
with scary situations temporarily. Through trial and error, they discover methods to push through challenges and survive tough circumstances. For example, some adults who are afraid to drive over
bridges white-knuckle their way across, breathing deeply, saying
affirmations, counting to ten repeatedly, or focusing only on the car
ahead of them. They get across, but their fear is just as palpable the
next time they are forced across a bridge. Their opinions and imag-
inings about bridges remain the same ("This is dangerous! I can't
do it!"), and they'll still try to avoid them whenever possible. These
types of strategies are designed to *get rid of* doubt or *suffer through*
discomfort. That's not a long-term solution.

The Big Picture Is Filled with Uncertainty

Fear, uncertainty, discomfort, worry . . . these are normal and
expected parts of life and are signs that you are moving forward,
stepping into life, and growing. But lots of anxious kids and parents don't see these feelings and sensations as normal. Instead, they
perceive them as powerful signals to *stop* and *avoid*. If this reaction
sounds like your family's, then it's one of the reasons you are stuck.

You and your child need to approach anxiety and anxiety-provoking situations with an altogether different attitude. We certainly have strategies—we've given you two already—but the seven puzzle pieces aren't just tips or techniques for getting through. Taken together, they're designed to shift your family out of that limiting, exhausting framework that comes with worry and to change your beliefs—and then your actions—regarding anxiety and risk.

In Chapter 4 we described the times when you can expect worry to arrive, and in Chapter 5 we offered some ways that you and your child can talk to worry when it shows up. These are the first shifts toward normalizing and then responding differently to worry's signals and demands. Now we go a step further: we want you and your child to get uncomfortable and uncertain—on purpose.

Believe us: We know how this sounds to you and your child. Day after day, hour after hour in our offices, we have relatively pleasant opening conversations with kids and parents. We're energetic and optimistic, and we talk about anxiety with confidence and calmness. We notice the bubbles of trust rising up. *This person understands our problem*, the faces say.

Then we eventually offer this proposal: "You've been working very hard to manage this anxiety thing, and you've gone to great lengths to keep everything as smooth and comfortable as possible in your house. But that's not working. I'm going to suggest some changes, and I'm going to ask you to be willing participants. We need to talk about how to become uncomfortable. And uncertain."

This is when faces drop. Kids who have been sitting up on the edge of the couch now sink back into the cushions and defiantly cross their arms in front of them. Scowls. Pouts. Parents usually hold more subtle expressions, but the small furrow between their brows conveys a message like "You want us to do *what*? Why would we want to be more uncertain than we already are? How does being *more* uncomfortable help anything?"

You probably want a thorough explanation of our rationale for suggesting something so seemingly crazy, and we will give that to you, because you must understand this principle so that you can support your child as she moves forward. First, though, we give you information about how anxiety uses your need for certainty and comfort to grow stronger. Then we explain why—in order to manage new and scary activities—you need to *honestly be willing* to feel those discomforts. In the next chapter we talk about how to change the way anxious brains act and different ways to reset the brain's alarm system. Together these two chapters crystallize the third puzzle piece: BE UNSURE AND UNCOMFORTABLE ON PURPOSE.

Be Unsure
and Uncomfortable
on Purpose

A TALE OF TWO PERSPECTIVES

All of the different types of anxiety depend on a few common processes to feed them. They need us to hold on to excessive, catastrophic, or unreasonable beliefs about the likelihood of an event going badly, and to focus excessively on negative consequences that could occur. In other words, anxiety lives within people who tend to see their world as a dangerous place, to imagine bad events happening with frequency, and to imagine those bad events leading to horrible results. These beliefs and the often-vivid imaginations that go along with them cause people to overscan the environment in order to identify and prevent danger, a process known as hypervigilance. "I'd better stay on top of this! I had better keep my guard up!" Anxiety *loves* and *feeds off* of hypervigilance.

But there's more. Fueled by our desire to prevent bad outcomes by avoiding any risk of danger, anxiety also depends on our learning nothing positive when we do face our fears. It's as if the anxious belief ("Something horrible is going to happen!") stays rigid and strong, even when, over and over, the actual evidence says otherwise. This is quite a trap. How can you learn to handle your fear—and adjust your predictions of impending, inevitable catastrophe—if you don't learn anything from positive experiences? When nothing bad or dangerous occurs, anxious people don't say to themselves, *Geez, this turned out fine. Maybe I didn't have to worry so much after all. Maybe I overreacted to my imagined threat of danger.* Instead, their fears and hypervigilance are reinforced and strengthened: "Good thing I was so careful! I protected my family, myself, and my children from harm." Anxious people focus on the wrong explanations, like a baseball player who improves his hitting and gives all the credit to his lucky socks instead of his diligent practice. Reinforcing hypervigilance also means employing the wrong strategies and making the wrong adjustments, all toward the goal of eliminating risk and avoiding any chance of a bad outcome.

Renee, for example, is terrified of being attacked in her neighborhood as she waits for the bus to go to work. Convinced that it is a dangerous time and place, she imagines getting beaten and left alone, bleeding on the sidewalk. So, when she goes to the bus each morning, she keeps her hand on her pepper spray and constantly scans the people around her. She tightens every muscle in her body, her heart beating and her neck craned. She is never attacked or even bothered, and she attributes this to her vigilant safety precautions, despite her husband's frequent reminders that the crime rate in her neighborhood is nearly zero. One day, Renee learns that a coworker's cousin was pickpocketed on the bus in another part of the city. That evening she tells her husband she is no longer taking the bus to work. Without another "safe" transportation alternative, Renee calls in sick for a week, then quits her job.

Here's another scenario to consider. Marybeth moves to a large city to attend graduate school. She has a few acquaintances there but will be living alone. She does a bit of research ahead of time and finds an apartment in a relatively safe and busy area near a well-lit subway stop.

One day after classes, Marybeth stops on the way home for a few groceries. When she takes her backpack off to get her wallet, the zipper is open, her wallet gone. Without any money, she leaves her groceries behind and cancels her credit cards when she gets back to her apartment. The next afternoon, she skips class and spends a few miserable hours at the Department of Motor Vehicles replacing her driver's license. She tells a classmate about it the next day. Her fellow student responds sympathetically, "Yeah, same thing happened to me last semester. They target women students with backpacks on the subway. Keep your wallet in your front pocket, and you'll be fine." Marybeth nods, having already made the switch. She also holds her backpack in front of her on the subway from then on.

Life is uncertain. People sometimes do get attacked, and many women choose to carry pepper spray and stay alert in unfamiliar environments. Crimes occur more often in some areas, but living in a safer section of town is no guarantee of security; it just lowers the risk. Public transportation means that you're with a lot of people in close quarters, so there's certainly a chance of getting your wallet stolen, especially if you leave it easily accessible in the pack on your back.

Not surprisingly, Marybeth worried as she hurried back to her apartment from the grocery store, since someone had her personal information and her credit cards. But she took steps to handle the problem. She felt uncomfortable that next day on the subway and at the DMV. But she accomplished her tasks nonetheless, and she stayed in school.

Let's zoom ahead several years. Imagine that fourteen-year-old Gwyneth wins a scholarship to take classes at a music school in another part of her large city. She can take a public bus from the high school to the music school, and then a parent can pick her up after class. This is a brand-new experience, and, although Gwyneth is excited, she's understandably nervous about a lot of changes. Will she do well at the classes? What if she isn't good enough? Will she know anyone? How will she figure out where to go? What will it be like to take the bus?

Take a moment to imagine Gwyneth is Renee's daughter. Now imagine Marybeth is her mom. What would each of these mothers say to Gwyneth about her upcoming adventure? What stories would each of them tell her? When Gwyneth says she's nervous and worried, and wonders out loud how she'll manage, what advice would each mother offer? What strategies? How about you? Would your parenting style be like Renée's ("The world is a dangerous place") or like Marybeth's ("As you spread your wings, be safe").

Anxiety demands certainty and comfort. But you need to support the inevitability of uncertainty and discomfort as your child grows.

Do you see what this means? To grow, your child *must* expect to feel anxious and worried from time to time.

If you've been playing by anxiety's rules—providing certainty and comfort to get through the school day, the bedtime routine, or the doctor's appointment—then rejecting its rules is the only way to move your family out of anxiety's grip. When you are willing to embrace feeling uncertain and getting uncomfortable, then you are on the right path.

Our first piece of the puzzle was to expect worry. You've probably already figured out that when you worry, you should also expect to feel anxious. Now we are adding action into the equation: to win over anxiety, we have to act courageously—to feel uncertain and uncomfortable . . . and step forward anyway.

> To grow, your child *must* expect to feel anxious
> and worried from time to time.

How do you make such a shift? How do you get your child to see the importance of being uncertain and uncomfortable, and to accept it as part of growing? First, you must pay attention to what you model for your child about handling uncertainty and risk. Next, you need to recognize and address the use and misuse of crutches: the ways in which you and others may be helping your child to avoid new or challenging situations. Let's start with role modeling and how you might be inadvertently teaching your child to avoid instead of acting courageously.

A Role Model Is Worth
a Thousand Words

Research tells us convincingly that your own relationship with anxiety and uncertainty—and how you role model this in front of your child—significantly impacts how she sees the world. Adults are routinely faced with situations that require us to step into uncertainty: leaving one job for another, moving to a new state, choosing a spouse, and, of course, raising children. Think for a few moments about the many decisions you make on a regular basis. Some are simple ("What should we have for dinner?") and some more complex ("Should I look for a different job? Should I stay in this relationship? Do I need to talk to my son's teacher or let him handle it on his own? Which car is a better purchase? Do we spend extra money on that vacation this year or wait?"). How do you handle these situations? What are you modeling during these decision-making processes?

People who seek certainty as their highest priority look for the one correct, positively perfect answer; decisions for those people can become time-consuming and overwhelming. Imagine for a moment that you are contemplating a job change. You can always ask more questions and gather more information. Even then it's impossible to predict the future. Therefore, if you are seeking guarantees, you tend to stay put. You might decide to forget about that new job, even though the pay is better and it's closer to home. It's an opportunity, but what if you accept and then don't really like it? What if it becomes too challenging? Best to leave well enough alone. Too risky.

What if complete safety isn't your top priority? You decide to go through the interview process, and you ask questions and hear answers that convince you that you could handle the job. It will be an adjustment, but after thinking about it and talking with people you trust, you accept the position. Do you feel some discomfort? Absolutely, with a whole new routine, different coworkers, and the loss of some close colleagues. Risk? Of course! But you accept that being uncomfortable and feeling challenged is part of moving ahead in your profession. You enjoy most aspects of your new job, and the pay raise feels great.

What might your child learn from you about this type of decision? Think about the attitude that each of the following responses illustrates:

- "I really don't like my current job. It's so boring. There's an opening at XYZ Company. I have no idea what it would be like there. At least here I know what to expect. Joan told me I should interview, but even thinking about it makes me nervous. I'm staying put."
- "I could stay at my job, but it's worth checking out XYZ Company. It's better pay, and it sounds like a more interesting job. I think I'll send over my résumé and see what happens."

Imagine that three months after taking the new job, your supervisor—the impressive person who interviewed you and offered you the job—leaves the company. Her replacement is disorganized and gruff. If he had been at the initial interview, you tell yourself, you wouldn't have taken the job. You like the increased pay, and some of the people you work with are great. But you sometimes wish you could have seen into the future and known of your supervisor's departure. Impossible, of course.

If your child were listening in on your response to this outcome, he might hear two possible reactions. What might he learn about handling change from each of these?

- "I can't believe my supervisor, Paula, left. I knew I should have stayed at my other job. What a bad decision I made! See, I'm just not good at making decisions."
- "Geez, my new supervisor is a bummer. I wish I had known that Paula was going to leave, but *she* didn't even know, she told me. At the time, I made a good decision to take the job. Now I'll have to deal with this issue. I'll figure it out, I guess. I do like the extra money and the project I'm working on."

You make heaps of decisions throughout your life that have uncertain outcomes. When you get into a car, you are engaging in one of daily life's riskiest endeavors. If you ever went to graduate school or interviewed for a job, asked someone to marry you or accepted someone's proposal, brought home a rescue dog or let your teenager get his driver's license, you probably acknowledged the risk, stepped into the uncertainty of the future, and handled whatever was going to happen next. It's scary, we know, but it is how we all grow and move our lives forward.

Believing that your task in life is to eliminate or control all risk for yourself or your anxious child perpetuates the fearful stance that says, "Stop! You can't handle this!" You might feel less threatened, but your family's world will become a lot smaller. If you only teach your children how to remain safe and comfortable, and if you pre-empt any difficulties coming toward them, then they will have no experience with or confidence in using their own abilities to manage problems. Preventing uncertainty and scanning for ways to avoid is only one way to respond to life as it unfolds in front of you.

Accepting uncertainty and then problem solving in new situations is an approach that you and your kids can master, but you have to give your children a chance to practice. Uncertainty and discomfort need to become normal and natural parts of your life rather than scary possibilities to be avoided at all costs—which is impossible, of course, and makes anxiety worse. You need not continually remind your child about the dangerous world out there. Instead, look for opportunities to support and normalize your child's willingness to take reasonable, beneficial, and sometimes uncomfortable risks. We encourage you to reflect this stance: "Yes, give it a try. Along the way, you'll learn to handle the stumbling blocks."

When we talk to kids, we tell them stories of regular folk and famous people who stepped into the unknown and grew from it. You should also tell such stories. Abraham Lincoln faced great uncertainty and risk when he pushed for the passage of the Thirteenth Amendment to end slavery. A century later, Rosa Parks didn't know what would happen when she refused to give up her seat in the front of the bus. A boy we know with cerebral palsy signed up to receive a service dog and traveled to another state to take a two-week training, not knowing if he'd be able to master his new responsibilities. He made it through, received his coveted dog, and now has vastly increased his territories of independence.

A girl we once knew was terrified of getting stung by a bee, so she stayed in her house as much as possible. But when she finally became willing to accept the possibility that she might get stung, and willing to be uncertain about what could happen—and even willing to be uncomfortable from a sting—then she was able to go play outside. Ultimately, when she did get stung, she handled it with a few tears, an ice pack, and a Popsicle.

Each of these people acted with the approach "I'm willing to be uncertain and uncomfortable because this is important to me. I want this outcome strongly enough that I'm willing to not know exactly what's going to happen." And each of them exhibited courage, according to our definition.

Courage

Be willing to feel unsure and uncomfortable,
and then step into the unknown.

Courage in our line of work is when the goal is important enough that you *willingly* move forward even when you're not sure how it's going to turn out, or when you predict you're going to feel uncomfortable. Families who are learning to handle anxiety in a different way must be courageous every day, so we suggest you post this formula for courage in some prominent spot in your home. Celebrating courage in little and big ways can motivate and inspire each of you to keep moving forward.

We also suggest that you look for opportunities to model this process for your children. Talk to them about how you moved toward uncertainty and how you handled it. Share stories such as, "I wasn't sure how to get there, but I made only a few wrong turns and I finally found my way," or "Boy, I was nervous about giving blood today, but I know there's a blood shortage, so I did it!" Illustrate to them frequently that you're not always sure how events will go, but you'll figure it out.

Here's another benefit when kids and parents loosen up their demand for certainty and start embracing all the facets of experience: our children experience success as problem solvers, and new activities become easier for them. Remember from Chapter 2 the research that showed how teaching kids to problem solve reduces the chance that they will develop an anxiety disorder? When families stop focusing on what bad might happen and stop planning for every eventual disaster, imaginations within the family are free to explore creative solutions and adventures. When we promote problem solving in our families, then we teach our children to *think* when facing a difficult event rather than simply reacting with panic and avoidance.

To help your children build their inner strength, you need to look at how they currently lean on supports that keep them dependent at the very times when they need to grow a sense of independence. We use the term "crutches" to label the ways that children restrict their activities in order to stay safe. When children lean on crutches repeatedly, they reinforce their belief, "I can't handle this on my own." Instead of facing new adventures, children use crutches to offer them multiple ways to avoid them.

Next we address the common use of crutches at home and at school. All of us use crutches to support ourselves. But we distinguish between crutches that help us expand our territories versus crutches that constrict us. We also talk about what you need to do differently, because parents can unknowingly become a crutch based on how they respond to their children's distress.

LEAN ON ME . . . JUST NOT THAT MUCH, PLEASE

What do you do when an upper shelf is just out of reach? Do you grab a stool or ask for help from that taller guy? How about when you're ready to buy a new car but you're having trouble sorting out the pros and cons of the many choices? Do you take guidance from *Consumer Reports*? What if you aren't confident negotiating with that salesperson? Do you ask cousin Vinnie to be your wingman as you haggle with the dealership?

When we doubt our ability to handle a task, we automatically start looking for support. That's completely normal and expected.

Our kids operate just like us: they create strategies to keep new or uncomfortable activities from overwhelming them. For instance, the first time your child spends the night at a friend's house, he may call you three or four times during the evening "just to check in." Those few calls help him to stay all night and then proudly say the next morning, "I did it!"

The skill of reaching out for support is quite handy as our children tackle new adventures. It allows them to feel more secure when they take risks and to develop a sense of personal control as they move through each new stage of development. Nightlights, blankets, and stuffed toys are all examples of crutches that young children use in a normal and helpful way.

But there is a downside to such reaching out for support. As soon as the need to feel in control and secure consistently becomes the top priority, a crutch is no longer a normal part of developing and growing. When seeking security becomes more important than exploring—when kids start to hesitate, to become dependent on others, and to back away from adventures—then we have a problem.

Obviously none of us wants our children to suffer. But our kids need to push through their insecurities, not get rid of them. If we act on our desire to remove their pain, we slide down that slippery slope of trying to eliminate their insecurities instead of teaching them how to be courageous. Before we know it, we're driving them to school instead of helping them take the bus, we're sitting in their bedrooms every single night until they've fallen asleep (like Janet did with her daughter Christie at the start of the chapter), or we're giving them our moment-by-moment schedules when we leave home to run an errand.

Crutches literally support us when we are weak, often while we recover or build up strength. Sounds good, right? Not so in the world of worry, because over time the dependence on worry crutches tends to increase rather than decrease. Continually leaning on crutches actually *strengthens* anxiety. How? Every time we use a crutch, we mentally review the danger lurking around the corner, and we attribute our ability to handle the danger to the *external* crutch rather than our own *internal* coping abilities.

For example, a child thinks, *Mom has to wait in the hall until I get settled in class. Because if she doesn't, I could get terribly anxious and need her, and she wouldn't be there, and I'd fall apart.* And then the child *demands* that Mom serve as her crutch. So Mom agrees to wait outside the classroom door for fifteen minutes before she leaves. Nothing goes wrong. No panic. No screaming child running out of the class and clinging to Mom. What does the child conclude? He doesn't think, *Hey, see that? I* can *stay in the classroom without falling apart.* When everything goes well and he has no distress, he concludes, *Boy, good thing Mom stayed outside the door. I could have really had trouble if she had left!* Parents might come to the same conclusion. *He did well today. I'm glad I stayed. My presence really helped him manage.* Worry crutches strengthen worry. They don't strengthen children.

All kids use supportive objects and people from time to time. Some supports help them successfully move through a new developmental phase, and others hold them back by causing them to doubt themselves. As we focus on the importance of stepping into new territories, your job is to learn the difference between the supports that help and those that hinder. Just as any physical therapist teaches a patient to move from bed to walker to full mobility after knee surgery, you must be willing to move your child away from the crutches that anxiety demands. Toward what? Independence. And just as those first steps after knee surgery feel uncomfortable and even scary, you both initially feel unsure and unsteady while you practice and integrate new strengths.

As you are reading this book and moving through life with your child, pay attention to the crutches you have in place that support anxiety's agenda. Technology, for example, has allowed crutches to become moment-to-moment strengtheners of anxiety. Children who are fearful of riding the bus home from school ("Other kids might be mean, the bus driver could miss my stop, you might not be home when I get off, I could leave my books on the seat") are given cell phones and can call a parent repeatedly along the bus route (or even stay connected to Mom the whole time, if desired). Anxious parents often promote the use of the phone to make sure their children are safe. We've had several parents who require a child to text every fifteen or thirty minutes when away from home. This approach tells the child, "I need to know where you are and what you're doing, and I must participate and approve of all the small decisions you're making throughout your day." Before you intervene in your child's struggles, ask yourself, *Am I promoting independence? Or am I encouraging dependence?*

One college student we know went to a meeting with her professor to discuss a disappointing grade on a paper and kept her mom secretly connected on the cell phone throughout the conversation. The mother, from 300 miles away, spoke up and began asking questions, much to the surprise of the unsuspecting professor. Another parent of a seven-year-old boy decided to give him a cell phone so he could text her while he was at playdates. This anxious family had been working hard at successfully changing their old accommodating patterns but initially didn't see this strategy as a crutch. As Mom explained the cell phone plan during their session, her son began asking repeatedly, "But what if there's no service at my friend's house? What if the phone doesn't work?" Worry was back in charge.

Here are some examples of crutches. They are neither good or bad until we view them in the context in which they are used.

Actions	People	Things
Calling parent when away from home	*Primary caregiver or parent*	*Nightlight or blanket*
Eliciting certain promises, like parent staying home during school hours	*Certain babysitter*	*Over-the-counter medications (Tylenol, Advil, cough syrup)*
Parents describing exactly where they will be	*Relative or sibling*	*Special toy, stuffed animal*
Parent calling in to school or looking into classroom	*Teacher/coach*	*Certain foods/ drinks*
Staying with school nurse or guidance coun-selor	*Best friend*	*Inhaler*
Sleeping with parents in the bed or on the floor	*Counselor/nurse*	*Cell phone*

SCHOOLS, ACCOMMODATION PLANS, AND CRUTCHES

When we are called in to consult with schools, we frequently discover that the school's accommodation plan for an anxious child actually *supports* worry. The goal in a school setting is to ensure that learning occurs, and we've already talked about how anxiety stops growth, experimenting, and curiosity. But, like well-meaning parents, schools often do their best to eliminate the sources of anxiety (short-term) and unknowingly create crutches throughout the school day that maintain anxiety in the long-term. The biggest crutch they insert into the child's day? Avoidance.

Take Laney, for example. Laney was worried about two experiences: loud noises and other children misbehaving. That made second grade tricky because children interacting in the cafeteria, gym class, and recess can be loud and unpredictable. A few boys in her class routinely had to sit out during gym because of their rowdy behavior. Coupled with the threat of monthly fire drills, Laney had a hard time getting much done, and she was soon making more and more visits to the nurse's office with a stomachache. Laney's teacher saw her teary eyes and avoidant behavior, and she wanted to help. With the goal of making Laney feel better and calmer, they came up with a plan: Laney was to go see the guidance counselor, Mrs. Dillon, whenever she felt worried or scared. She could "rest" there until she felt ready to return to the classroom. The school also agreed that if Laney felt unable to handle an activity at school and was too distressed to return to her classroom, her mom could pick up Laney early.

The crutches—visits to the guidance office, calls home, avoidance of certain environments, and early pickups—helped Laney to escape her fears and feel more comfortable. But since no one was showing Laney how to handle her worries, the frequency of visits and pick-ups increased, and Laney began checking in at the front office each morning to make sure the guidance counselor was in school that day. As long as Laney knew Mrs. Dillon was in the building (and as long as she could have unlimited visits), she was cute and smiley. Everyone was pleased with the change in her demeanor. But when the guidance counselor slipped on the ice and broke her elbow, requiring her to be out for several weeks, Laney had no other independent coping strategies and refused to attend school at all until Mrs. Dillon was back on the job. When Mrs. Dillon—and Laney—finally did return to school, Laney had another worry added to the list: the health and well-being of Mrs. Dillon, now an essential crutch.

If you are working with your child's school, make sure that any accommodations have a weaning-off plan. Step by step, your child should be encouraged to move into challenges, not away from them. We worked with Laney's teacher and Mrs. Dillon on how to reach the best outcome. In Laney's case, the goal was to decrease the visits to Mrs. Dillon's office (her crutch), to stay in class more, and to eliminate early pickups. Laney, her parents, and her supports at school needed to learn how to expect worry, externalize it, and talk to it. Laney also needed to understand how her seemingly helpful crutches were making her anxiety stronger, and she needed an incentive to help change this pattern.

Laney and Mrs. Dillon created a worksheet that made a game of tracking what Laney's worry said (*Mrs. Dillon has to be in school, or I can't handle being here. Gym is too loud for me. What if we have a fire drill?*) and then what Laney said back (*Mrs. Dillon won't be here every single day, so I can learn how to get through my day even when she's absent. I don't like loud noises, but it's okay* not *to like them and handle them at the same time. Fire drills are supposed to be loud and startling so that we listen and move out of the building. I can put my hands over my ears if I want to and still follow the directions.*).

Laney's Plan for Handling School

When did worry show up, and what did it say?	What did I say to worry?	How did I make myself uncomfortable?	What happened?
I had gym today, and worry said that Dylan and Scott were going to be too loud.	I don't like loud kids, but I can handle their noise. They might have to sit, but that's okay with me!	I went to gym, even though I wanted to go see Mrs. Dillon.	Dylan was loud, but Scott was absent. I played floor hockey a little bit, and I stayed in gym the whole time. I was okay.
I worried about a fire drill. Worry said it was going to happen today, so I shouldn't go to the bathroom.	I have to go the bathroom, and if there's a fire drill, I'll be scared, but I know what to do.	I went to the bathroom! Twice!	There wasn't a fire drill after all. I felt good because I didn't put worry in charge. I was nervous in the bathroom, but I went.
I wanted to know if Mrs. Dillon was here today, and worry said go check in her office.	Mrs. Dillon might be here. If she's not here, I can handle it. Sometimes Mrs. Dillon will be absent, and that's normal.	I didn't go check for Mrs. Dillon, and I didn't ask my teacher if Mrs. Dillon was here.	Mrs. Dillon was here. I saw her in the hall after art class. It's okay to be happy when I see her and to miss her when she's absent, but I can handle it.

Mrs. Dillon and Laney's classroom teacher coached Laney that being uncomfortable was not only okay, it was *helpful*. She had to feel uncomfortable if she wanted to defeat her worries and handle school with more confidence. Unexpected events like fire alarms and broken elbows happen sometimes, and even rowdy kids in gym class certainly happen, too.

The messages Laney heard from adults around her changed, and thus Laney gave herself different messages, too.

- *Original message from adults*: "Laney can't handle noise or unpredictability. She's fragile and gets upset, so let's make sure we keep her feeling safe by giving her an escape plan."
- *Revised message*: "Laney gets uncomfortable with loud noises and bad behavior, but she can learn to handle these events and her own worries as well. When Laney has a better internal strategy, she can manage what happens in school rather than fleeing."

You now have a better understanding of how adults strengthen anxiety, sometimes in themselves and sometimes in children. We know from years of experience that few people actually have this information, so if you and the other adults in your child's life have been seeking out comfort and supporting your child with crutches, you're in good company. You also now know why it doesn't work.

Instead, we are encouraging you and your family to find ways to become unsure and uncomfortable on purpose, looking for opportunities, large or small, where you can practice tolerating doubt and distress. Those arenas will be where each of you grow.

We have more to share on the topic of uncertainty and discomfort. It's time to learn how to retrain the anxious brain that has become so skilled at avoidance. As Laney's story illustrates, understanding about anxious worrying and then shifting your attitude about it are the important first steps in the process. But being willing to push into new territory is a huge next step for most families. Next we're going to explain the necessity of taking action while uncomfortable. You're going to learn how experience—and only experience—resets the primitive alarm system that has been making unchecked anxiety so powerful within your family.

TIME TO TAKE ACTION:
Applying the Concepts of Chapter 6

Just for Parents

What crutches are you providing for your child? How is the school providing crutches? What are you doing that fosters your own or your child's avoidance? Spend some time thinking about how these crutches also help you feel more comfortable as a parent.

Use the form below to list any crutches that your child may be using in uncomfortable situations. Remember that the crutches can be actions, people, and things.

Event	Crutches

Model the Process . . .
of Accepting and Moving Toward
Discomfort and Uncertainty

Look for opportunities to model a willingness to tolerate doubt and distress. Share with your children how you moved toward uncertainty and how you handled it. Mention any daily events like, "I had to handle that Friday traffic today and I thought I was going to be late, but I made it," or "Someone cut in front of me in line at the grocery store, and even though I was nervous I spoke up!" Also talk about important moments in your life when you used your courage to move toward a change, like moving away from home, joining a group when you knew no one, or any situation in which you felt unsure but took a risk and solved a problem.

Use caution with how you tell the stories. Sensitive kids may pick up on a critical tone. You should not imply, "Why can't you do it this way?" Instead, build rapport by conveying how insecure someone can feel before an event and then share how pushing through insecurity can lead to a successful outcome.

Retraining the Brain:
Doing Matters Most

If you hear a voice within you say,
"You cannot paint," then by all means paint,
and that voice will be silenced.

—VINCENT VAN GOGH

We learn by doing. Bottom line: If you want to learn to swim, at some point you're going to have to get into the water. You can lie on the living room rug and move your limbs, turn your neck out of the pretend water, and take a breath of the pretend air, as you pretend float and sink. But no Red Cross lifeguard is going to pass you along in swim lessons because you can pretend to swim on the carpet. You have to get into the water, and you have to be willing to thrash around a bit, to feel awkward, to suck some real water into your real nose, and to do some real sinking and floating and frantic grabbing for the edge of the pool. This is called experiential learning. You move along, through experience, from not being able to perform a task to being competent at the task. Simple.

Anxiety tries to get in the way of experiential learning by saying, "Don't try!" and "It'll end terribly!" and "You can't handle this!" We have been encouraging you to act opposite of these messages, to step forward into unfamiliar territory, to actually seek out uncertainty and the distress it generates within you. In this chapter, we explain why and how this new attitude of "I'm willing to be unsure and uncomfortable" must team up with the doing of experiential learning to retrain the brain. This combination of attitude and action helps the brain to learn and relearn, to create different responses. Being willing to learn to swim but unwilling to get wet won't work. Getting into the pool but clutching the edge with no intention of experimenting with the swim coach's instructions won't work either. We must have intention as well as action.

Brains are magnificent, complicated structures. Our goal here is to explain how anxiety and the brain work—and how to manage them—in a way that makes sense to you and your child. For our purposes, we focus on the amygdala and the prefrontal cortex; kids' terms for these parts of the brain might be the "alarm system" and "the thinking part." The parents and children we work with tend to welcome this information. When kids can understand what's happening inside their brains and bodies, they are less overwhelmed by their thoughts and physical sensations. Not surprisingly, most of the kids we see have no knowledge of how the worried brain works. With a bit of education and some drawings about the brain, children are far more willing and even excited to do what we ask them to do.

The amygdala (uh-MIG-duh-luh) is a little almond-shaped structure in the brain (actually two almonds, side-by-side), and its job is to activate an emergency response. Think of it as one big panic button. If we signal the amygdala that a threat is in close proximity, the amygdala activates. Efficiently and reliably, it gets to work, sending out messages to trigger the body's defense systems. Part of the trigger is generated by epinephrine (also known as adrenaline), which is secreted within the brain and from the adrenal glands, which sit on top of the kidneys.

When entering the bloodstream, epinephrine is carried around the body to various locations where it initiates several aspects of the fight-or-flight response. Epinephrine's effects have a collective purpose: to provide energy so that the major muscles of the body can respond to the perceived threat. When animals are in danger, this response is terrific. A threatened grizzly bear, cat, or chipmunk automatically goes into a mode of protection—fighting, fleeing, or sometimes becoming perfectly frozen—depending on the animal and the circumstances.

When we humans need the same response, it's there in a flash. It can get triggered while playing at recess (a foot slips off the ladder of the slide) or at the start of a class (*My teacher is holding a set of papers. Is this a pop quiz? I didn't read the chapter!*). But if you are sensitive to anxiety, what happens next? Lots of kids and adults get scared of feeling scared and try not to get scared again. That's the response we need to change. Otherwise, we continue to reinforce a negative pattern: anxiety leads to more anxiety, and then leads to avoidance. To figure out what to do, let's look at another part of the brain that becomes active during a threat.

The prefrontal cortex is located in the very front of the brain, just behind the forehead, and is in charge of many vital aspects of human functioning. It allows us to plan ahead, create strategies, and adjust our reactions when the environment changes around us. It helps us to focus our thoughts, pay attention, learn, and concentrate on our goals. The prefrontal cortex is in charge of abstract thinking and analysis, helping to regulate our behavior by managing conflicting thoughts, making choices between right and wrong, and predicting

the probable outcomes of different actions. That's a lot of responsibility. For our purposes, remember this: The prefrontal cortex is
responsible for taking in data through the body's senses, analyzing
the data, and deciding on actions.

So, the relationship between someone's prefrontal cortex and
her amygdala has a lot to do with anxiety, panic, and avoidance. It
accounts for all those screaming temper tantrums when your child
doesn't want to participate in an event that is new or feels scary. And
it comes down to this: the prefrontal cortex—when it decides that
an event is a threat—keeps sending those danger messages to the
amygdala, and thus the ever-cooperative amygdala keeps firing up
the alarm system.

Does it matter that the situation isn't really dangerous? Not to the
amygdala. It's a very primitive structure, simply doing what it's told.
Think of it like a smoke detector. When there's smoke it beeps loudly.
It doesn't politely beep and say, "Hey, Reid, you're burning a bagel
again!" It doesn't reserve a different, more urgent type of beep to
signal if the basement is on fire. For the smoke detector, smoke
means "sound the alarm," regardless of the source or amount of the
smoke. For the amygdala, a danger message means sound the alarm,
even if the danger is more imagined than real. Therefore, unchecked
worried thoughts and how we imagine events going wrong both set
off the alarm system. Plus, if you are *afraid* of the thoughts and sensations that your alarm system sets off, you set off your alarm system
again. Fear sets off the amygdala.

> If you tell yourself there is a threat, even though there
> is no threat, your body and mind sound the alarm.

If your child repeatedly tells herself that a situation is dangerous, then she is signaling the amygdala repeatedly to fire off an anxiety (fight-or-flight) response. And if she's been afraid of the fight-or-flight response, she'll automatically intensify that response. *Something* has to change here.

Consider the example of someone taking a commercial airplane flight. Turbulence is completely safe for the plane. But if the plane passes through some turbulence, and if this person interprets the turbulence as dangerous, then the amygdala sets off its alarm. To stop becoming so frightened by turbulence, he can stop flying. Problem solved. But if he wants the convenience of air travel, his other choice is to change his interpretation.

Here are two possible conversations that illustrate how we might internally handle worry or fear. Pay attention to the process of activating and escalating the alarm system.

✳ ✳ ✳

Sylvia is taking her first commercial flight today. As she boards the plane, she's worried about whether she can cope with this new experience, and she starts talking to herself. Her amygdala, like any good alarm system, is listening in for signals, ready to respond at literally a moment's notice.

Sylvia [*talking to herself*]: Oh, I don't know about this. I can't handle this. It's too much for me. I want to get out of here. I've never done this before.

Amygdala [*listening in*]: What? There's danger? I'll protect us. I'll get our heart beating and our muscles ready to run. I'll release some epinephrine and get ready for an emergency. [Of course, the amygdala doesn't really talk. But go with it, please.]

SYLVIA [*reacting fearfully to her body's arousal*]: Well, now I'm feeling worse. My body isn't feeling right. Heart pounding, sweaty. This is too much. I knew I couldn't handle this. I really have to calm down, but I can't. What is my body doing? I'm going to lose it!

AMYGDALA: What's that? More panic messages! We're in danger, right? Come on, body and mind, get ready to run or fight in just a moment.

SYLVIA [*still interpreting the body's arousal as a threat to her*]: It's getting worse. I have to get out. My body feels terrible. I'm feeling nauseated. I'm afraid of this airplane, and my body is out of control, too!

AMYGDALA: Alarm system on! Danger!

SYLVIA: I can't handle this! What am I going to do? I'm trapped! [More danger messages . . .]

✳✳✳

Is there a more beneficial way to conduct this inner dialogue? Yes. The latest research tells us that when you seek out discomfort and uncertainty, you can diminish anxiety. How? By resetting the amygdala, the alarm center of the brain. When confronted with the unknown, worriers talk to themselves in a way that sets off the alarm center. The worrier says, "Oh, no!" The amygdala says, "Danger!" And the body responds accordingly. When this happens repeatedly, the fight-or-flight alarm center develops a bit of a hair trigger. The result? Lots of false alarms, lots of fear, and then lots of backing away from activities in order to feel safe and comfortable again. When you face these same challenging situations using a new set of skills—like voluntarily and purposely seeking out uncertainty and discomfort—you can quiet down the amygdala and generate fewer false alarms.

So let's try this same scene again—Sylvia's first time on a plane—although she now talks to herself in a different way. She interrupts that danger message, and the alarm system backs off:

SYLVIA [*talking to herself*]: I'm not so sure about this. I've never done this before. Maybe this was a bad idea. Now I'm stuck on this plane, but I feel like I need to get out of here.

AMYGDALA [*listening in*]: Wait, did you say "stuck"? Stuck is not good. I'll get us ready to escape. Give me a half second and I'll get the alarm system going. *All systems go!*

SYLVIA: Now I'm feeling weird. I'm all jittery.

AMYGDALA: Well, you had my attention when you announced, "I'm stuck." When you need to escape, that's my cue for action. *I'm here to save you!*

SYLVIA: I've never flown in a plane before, so I don't know exactly how it's going to go. That's why I'm worried, and I can feel my body getting worked up, too. But I really *want* to take a vacation, and I don't want to waste time driving. I'm nervous, but that's normal in this situation: I'm feeling scared of this new experience, that's all. I can handle feeling uncomfortable. I want to get to Florida, so I want to fly on this plane. If I *have* to feel uncomfortable to get through it, then I'm willing to feel uncomfortable. On the way back it probably won't be so hard.

AMYGDALA: So now you're saying you *want* to stay on the airplane? Oh, great. I've already set the alarm system in motion. I'm preparing for the escape. Now what?

SYLVIA: Being worried about this first flight is setting off a false alarm. That's why I'm so uncomfortable. But it's not an emergency. Actually, this is probably good practice for me. I need a little retraining.

AMYGDALA: Really? It's just that I've gotten used to jumping into action so quickly. . . . You mean this isn't quite so serious? Fine, I'll turn down the juice. Better?

SYLVIA: Hey! I feel a bit better already. Now I'm just going to breathe a bit. No escape needed. I can expect to feel uncomfortable here. It's part of the process. Heart beating a bit, butterflies in my stomach. But certainly not an emergency.

AMYGDALA: You seem to be handling this, so I can keep the major alarm system off. I'm clear about your message now. This is a new experience for you, but not an emergency. I'll keep you in "new experience" mode of arousal.

SYLVIA: Whew! That was close. I was feeling pretty uncomfortable for a bit. I got through it, though. That was pretty good practice!

AMYGDALA: We got through that, and I think we're okay. Now fasten your seat belt.

See the difference? In the first conversation, Sylvia's alarming self-talk sets off the amygdala. Then she amplifies the reaction, freaking out because the alarm system is going off. Body tight. Engine racing. In the second conversation, Sylvia expects to have some worries and be uncomfortable. She reminds herself—remember, the amygdala is listening—of this important fact: while being uncomfortable and uncertain is a normal part of this new situation, setting off a serious alarm response is *not* necessary. The amygdala decides, "I can take this down a notch. It's not a crisis." When Sylvia slows down, she sends different messages. Without a full-blown panic, she can manage the situation.

Children frequently ask us a reasonable question: "If my amygdala is causing all these alarms, why don't I just have it removed?" We explain that the amygdala is crucial to our survival. It gets the body going when there is *real danger*, so we do indeed need it. Real danger most often triggers the amygdala through an instantaneous (three-millisecond) fast track from the brain's thalamus. (The prefrontal cortex sends messages on the slow track; it might take a whole second to respond.) In other words, we can generate an emergency response without even being consciously aware of it. If your car hits a patch of ice and begins to slide, you're going to want that emergency response to keep you from slamming into the ditch. When a foul ball comes whizzing right toward your head as you sit in the bleachers, you had better hope your amygdala responds in that three milliseconds so you can duck.

So we'll keep that amygdala, thank you. But if you're a worrier, it's going to need some retraining. You need to stop sending those unwarranted danger messages through your prefrontal cortex, which means changing your perspective on which events are really threatening versus events you can actually manage. Your amygdala needs a chance to figure out that the classroom, recess, the bedroom, or bumblebees are manageable. You help your amygdala learn by placing it in the fearful situation and allowing it to hang out there, uncontaminated by that worried prefrontal cortex and all of its *oh-no* messages. The amygdala then realizes the minimal threat and stops setting off the system-wide alarm. When your child consciously says (and believes), "I can handle this. . . . I'm willing to be unsure and uncomfortable. . . . I can expect my worry to show up and learn what to do. . . . It's okay to be nervous," the amygdala then learns over time not to go into fight-or-flight and not to secrete so much epinephrine.

It takes practice and repetition for the brain to learn, but given the opportunity to hear different responses, it will learn. Those of us who specialize in treating anxiety disorders have taken this approach for twenty years, and we know it works. We've successfully taught it to children as young as four years old, and we can teach it on these pages to you and your family.

In the last chapter we wrote,

> Some adults who are afraid to drive over bridges white-knuckle their way across, breathing deeply, saying affirmations, counting to ten repeatedly, or focusing only on the car ahead of them. They get across, but their fear is just as palpable the next time they are forced across a bridge. Their opinions and imaginings about bridges remain the same ("This is dangerous! I can't do it!"), and they'll still try to avoid them whenever possible. These types of strategies are designed to *get rid of* doubt or *suffer through* discomfort. That's not a long-term solution.

You should now have a better understanding of what's happening here. If you drive across the bridge while telling yourself how dangerous it is, your prefrontal cortex awakens your amygdala, and no new learning takes place. On the next bridge—calling up that same anticipatory dread, the same messages of danger, and the same alarms going off—you reinforce the same negative pattern.

How might you break this routine? You have lots of choices about the details, but four broad moves make up the process:

1. You have to *want* to learn a new way to respond.

2. Choose to put yourself in any situation that you believe is safe but will stimulate some degree of the threat you feel as you drive across that bridge.
3. Permit yourself to feel those anxious feelings. Allow those fearful thoughts to rise up, but maintain an overarching belief that you can handle this experience.
4. Hang out there.

You don't have to begin by driving over a bridge. What else gives you a similar feeling? Here are some examples:

If You're Afraid of This . . .	Will Any of These Make You Anxious?
Height of the bridge	*Walking across a bridge; riding in a glass elevator; leaning over a railing; riding as a passenger across a bridge*
Feeling trapped	*Travel while sitting in the middle of the backseat of a car, with someone on both sides of you; ride a crowded elevator; sit in the middle of the movie theater with a person on each side of you*
Uncomfortable physical sensations	*Breathe through a cocktail straw for one minute (suffocation); take fifteen deep breaths and exhale quickly (hyperventilation, dizziness, lightheadedness)*

If nothing else gives you a fearful sensation similar to driving over a bridge, then courageously drive over a bridge, but do it while practicing the attitude and action we are describing here.

Talking It Up, Floor by Floor

What is it like to apply this new point of view? Here's an illustration from one of our adult clients.

✳✳✳

Looking at her, no one would doubt that Susan is scared. Her hands are visibly shaking, and she's doing a little *I'm-not-sure-about-this* dance as we approach the elevator. Imagine it as a *two-steps-forward-one-step-back* kind of shuffle. She's afraid of closed-in spaces. For years now, to avoid those suffocating feelings, she has ducked into hundreds of stairways and avoided numerous plane flights. Today Susan is determined to face her "demons," as she calls them.

After we step on the elevator, she gives the nod that we can travel up one single floor together. Then, as the doors slide closed, Susan's shaky hands turn into full-body tremors, and tears spill down her bright red face.

Forty-five minutes later, a laughing, beaming Susan steps off the elevator onto the twelfth floor. She has ridden those dozen floors alone, round-trip, four times in these most recent ten minutes. Our job is done for today, and we head back to our office.

✳✳✳

Susan accomplished something impressive that afternoon. Equally significant is that this rapid change is now a common outcome for people who are prepared for such an adventure. Literally dozens of studies, looking at thousands of people who suffer from anxiety and phobias, have proven that if you are committed to taking back control of your life, we can get you there.

How did Susan move in just forty-five minutes from trembling at the site of a closed-in space to grinning broadly as she rides up and down in an eight-foot cube? As expected, we coached her for a bit in previous office sessions. It was the same coaching we're giving you and your child here: What will worry predictably say? What will you say back? We taught her also about the significance of the amygdala, the brain's alarm. By the time she was standing in front of the elevator that day, here are the principles she was determined to apply:

- My amygdala needs to learn that closed-in spaces might feel uncomfortably small, but they aren't inherently dangerous.
- To ensure that my amygdala has a chance to learn, I need to change my *opinion* about my automatic thoughts and feelings as I approach the elevator. The most helpful opinion sounds something like this: *It's fine to have scary thoughts right now. I'm* supposed *to be scared, because for years now, feeling trapped has made me physically and emotionally uncomfortable. I can handle these feelings.*
- If I allow myself to have these thoughts and feelings—if I can just notice them without running from them, fixing them, or getting rid of them—then I'm helping to train my amygdala.

And that's what she did. As that elevator door closed for the first time, and as we took that quick ride to the second floor, she let herself feel terrified—and terrified she was. We took a two-minute recuperation break on the second floor, then rode to Floor 3. Another two-minute break. Floor 4. Then Floor 5.

After ten minutes, even though she was still scared, she said, "I'm ready for a two-floor ride."

Think about this for moment: After only ten minutes of practicing, she was already learning to trust those principles. Why? Because once she was *willing* to be scared, she allowed her amygdala to learn. As soon as her amygdala started learning that there was no *true* threat, it stopped secreting so much epinephrine. Translation: Susan felt less anxious.

In the previous chapter, Laney learned to use the same principles. At first, her supportive statements didn't come automatically. As she headed to gym class or began wondering if Mrs. Dillon was okay, she talked to herself in a way that put her body on high alert. But over time, as she continued to go to school and to gym class, she trained herself to consciously subvocalize supportive messages as she took action: *I am going to gym because my prefrontal cortex [thinking part] and my amygdala [alarm system] need to learn that noisy boys are annoying but not dangerous to me.*

This is why self-talk and action *together* are so important. Your child has to step toward the threatening situation and let the amygdala hang out and learn. She will have fearful thoughts and feelings at first, but by reminding herself that she is retraining her amygdala, she becomes able to tolerate what's happening. She must remind her prefrontal cortex that this is the plan. Taking on this new attitude and stepping into the threat *must happen together*. She must purposely, voluntarily choose to be unsure and uncomfortable.

(By the way, we have learned that even very young children prefer the terms "prefrontal cortex" and "amygdala." We always offer the child-friendly alternatives as we teach kids about their brains, but very few use them. They want to use the more "sophisticated" names to educate other adults. Based on the fact that we are teaching kids mastery and confidence, we think this is very cool.)

Laney also learned about her brain. She drew pictures of her pre-frontal cortex sending different messages to her amygdala. She was able to talk to her parents and teachers about how to get uncomfortable in order to learn through experience. She needed support while making this complete change in strategy. Thus, Laney and Mrs. Dillon also kept track of when and how she stepped into discomfort, and talked about how repetition of this process helped her worry become weaker and retrained her amygdala. Like Susan in the elevator, Laney gained confidence in her own ability to get through fearful situations. Her meetings with Mrs. Dillon—scheduled less and less frequently—focused on learning new skills instead of serving as an avoidant crutch.

Many of the parents we meet have a hard time tolerating emotional intensity. They worry that by pushing their children, they are going to do irreparable harm. Remember this: pushing an anxious child into situations without any understanding or positive strategies often scares them and causes them to further resist you. Setting off the fight-or-flight response repeatedly with no plan or shift in beliefs doesn't work. We wouldn't push you unprepared into a deep pool if you couldn't swim, and we are not telling you to push your child without support in place. But we are telling you to consistently and calmly move your child toward uncertainty and independent problem solving by passing on the strategies we're sharing with you.

See Dog, Willingly Stand There, Repeat

Here's an example of how calmly moving your child toward uncertainty and independent problem solving might look and sound within a family. Anthony is a thirteen-year-old boy working on his fear of dogs. As you follow the story, pay attention to how Anthony

and his mom shift their stance, talk to the prefrontal cortex, and
retrain the amygdala.

✳✳✳

Three years ago, when Anthony was ten, a neighbor's dog
jumped at him and bit him in the face. His cheek was badly
torn, just missing his eye. After three surgeries, Anthony's
scars are barely noticeable, but he is now so frightened of all
dogs that he avoids many activities. He doesn't visit friends'
houses where dogs live, he refuses to play soccer at the park,
and recently he stopped going to his drum lessons because
his teacher has a dog. Whenever Anthony is out of the house,
he scans for dogs, using his parent as a shield whenever he
can. Anthony's mom hoped that his fear would lessen over
time, but she reports that it's grown stronger instead. When
Anthony and his mom first came to see us, this is what he
said: whenever he sees a dog or hears barking—or even
thinks about whether there might be a dog somewhere—his
heart pounds, he feels hot, and his stomach feels queasy.
When he thinks about dogs, he vividly recalls the day the dog
bit him, including the ambulance siren, blood all over him,
and his little brother screaming. He knows that he will feel
better if he stays away from dogs, but he worries that a dog
could show up anywhere, at any time. He feels best (safest)
when he stays at home.

During our session, we help Anthony understand what's
been happening in his brain and his body, the very same
information that this chapter explains to you. We want him
to see how his goal of avoiding all dogs actually makes his

fear stronger. We show him some drawings about how his internal reaction to dogs sets off his alarm and throws him into fight-or-flight. After about twenty minutes of discussion, Anthony explains how he perceives his current relationship with dogs: "I have to stay away from them. I don't want to get bitten again. That was very scary, and I need to make sure it never happens again. Dogs are not safe."

Anthony wasn't afraid of dogs before he was bitten. In fact, his family has always had a dog, and he's always liked them. He feels sad and almost guilty that he can't be around them. "I know that some dogs are nice. Sometimes I see a cute dog, like at my drum teacher's house, and I think I should pet him, but I'm too scared."

Anthony agrees that being around dogs again would make his life easier in many ways. He understands why this fear has remained so powerful, and now he wants to retrain his brain. We decide that he will start by going to his drum lesson and seeing his teacher's dog, Barney. Anthony knows that his worry will show up. It will tell him he can't go near Barney and vividly remind him of his dog bite. We write up a list of what we think will happen and what he'll do in response:

1. Go to Mr. Zimmer's house for drum lesson. Expect worry to come along, too.
2. Hear worry remind me that dogs bite, and that Barney is a dog.
3. Tell myself and my worry that it's okay to feel scared. It's normal. I can handle it.
4. Hear Barney's collar jingling as he comes to the door.
5. Tell my worry that I'm going to feel scared and nervous, but that's part of my brain retraining.

6. Notice that my stomach feels weird and my heart is pounding, and that's okay, too.
7. When Mr. Zimmer lets me in through the screen door, let Barney follow me to the music room.
8. Let my amygdala hang out with Barney, even if my worry tells me to run for it.
9. Say out loud, "I can handle being near Barney because I want to get over this fear. Worry wants me to run, but I'm resetting my alarm system. I'm standing here so that can happen."
10. Whenever I see or hear a dog when I'm out, go back to #2, just like with Barney. Repeat and repeat.

Anthony returns a few weeks later, list in hand. The first trip to Mr. Zimmer's was rough, he says. It took him a long time to get out of the car, and he really began to think this whole plan was stupid. Finally he went to the door, and when he entered the house, he let Barney sniff at his shoes. He was scared, but he survived. Several times over the next few weeks he heard dogs or went to the park and watched them run around with their owners. He kept his list in his pocket and reread it when he needed to. He had another drum lesson and actually gave Barney a little scratch on his ears.

Then something unexpected happened, Anthony says. He and his family decided to go on a hike up a nearby mountain. He figured he might see dogs, so he and his mom made a new updated list for the hike.

"I knew my worry was going to talk to me. It wanted me to remember the dog bite. We started hiking, and about halfway up, a dog came running down the trail. It wasn't on a leash. I froze, but then I told my worry that I was okay. The dog was wagging his tail. Not that big. I stood there and let my amygdala hang out. The dog ran by, and I was okay. And that kept happening! My mom said I was the luckiest kid on the planet . . . all that brain retraining. We counted dogs. We made it a game. Nine dogs came by us on that hike."

> It's not *possible* for kids to always feel secure. They will grow as they tolerate an uncertain outcome and step forward anyway.

Anthony comes for a few more sessions. We talk about how he can use his thinking brain—his prefrontal cortex—to be smart around dogs. Not all dogs are friendly, and some should be avoided, but he is able to analyze and decide without setting off his amygdala every time. Will he worry sometimes when he sees a big dog? Sure. Will he change his plans to avoid a threatening dog that he doesn't know? Absolutely. But he can go back to his normal activities knowing that he has a better plan to make these decisions.

***

Anthony was a wonderful client, but his story is no different from what we see over and over again in our offices. This is exactly what we want you to learn: once you and your child understand the importance of moving toward the risk, of talking to your brain in a different way, and letting your brain and body react and relearn, then your lives can improve quickly.

It's not possible for kids to *always* feel secure. They will grow as they tolerate an uncertain outcome and step forward anyway. If kids don't find a way to encourage themselves to step forward, they will either keep stepping back from challenging tasks or continually grab some crutch to make them feel secure.

The next chapter gives you some breathing skills that aid in quieting the amygdala and the worries of the prefrontal cortex so that you and your child can get back to work in a problem-solving way. While many people focus on relaxation as a primary treatment for anxiety, you may be a bit surprised to learn how we incorporate this next puzzle piece into our step-into-it approach. Or maybe, by this point, you won't be surprised at all.

TIME TO TAKE ACTION:
Applying the Concepts of Chapter 7

Just for Parents

It's likely that the information we've given you about the brain and its various functions is new to you, as it will be to your child. If you are anxious yourself or have a pretty strong fear of something, spend a few minutes thinking about how you go about setting off your alarm system. When moving toward a feared situation or trigger, what does your internal talk sound like? How quick are you to send a danger message to your brain? When you do set off your amygdala, how do you handle that response? Conversely, if you do well with self-talk under stressful or fearful circumstances, what do you say to yourself? Where did you learn to do this? How has it helped you?

Plant the Seeds of . . .
How "Alarm Systems" and "Thinking Parts"
Work in the World

Conversations about nature offer you opportunities to talk about how animals and humans respond to threat. Help your child learn about fight-or-flight by talking about or observing how animals handle dangerous situations and why a creature's alarm system is important to survival. Also observe how sometimes we humans set off alarms by mistake, and how our response to a problem might be bigger than needed. (We glance at a stick and think it's a snake; a car backfires, and we think it's someone shooting a gun.) Use these observations to help your child differentiate between helpful and unhelpful alarm responses.

Model the Process . . .
of Talking Down the Prefrontal Cortex

How is your self-talk? How do you respond to anxious sensations in your body? Remember that we talked about safety chatter in Chapter 5. Pay attention again to what you say and what you model for your child when you're anxious. Do you avoid situations? If you have to face one of your own anxiety-provoking events while you're with your child (you might even set one up on purpose), talk out loud just as Susan did in the elevator or Sylvia did on the plane. Tell your child how you're retraining your amygdala by moving into the situation and hanging out there. Hearing a parent talk through a fearful situation can make a powerful impression on a child. Seek out something minor that scares you but *not* your child (spiders? flying? heights?) and model the very strategies we want your child to learn.

Some phrases to use:

- "I know this scares me and sets off my amygdala, but I'm showing my amygdala that it's not dangerous."
- "My alarm system is going off, but I know it's just a false alarm."
- "Even though I don't like _____, when I tell my brain I can handle it, it stops acting like it's an emergency."

Calming Down the Body

After reading and working with Chapter 7, you can understand the importance of letting children feel uncomfortable as they move into new situations in order to help reset their amygdalae. Your child needs to face challenging situations using a new set of skills—including a willingness to feel the sensations and move through them—so that he will ultimately generate fewer false alarms.

That said, we also know that the physical symptoms of anxiety can be dramatic and frightening. Shaking, sweating, headaches, even vomiting and diarrhea, garner fearful attention and often lead to a more dramatic refusal of activities. Once a child has a strong physical reaction, she is even more determined to avoid the situation that triggered it, and who can blame her? Adults are no different: the idea of giving a speech in front of your colleagues may be scary, but if you vomit during the speech? Horrifying.

In this chapter, we offer some skills for managing these physical reactions. As your child steps into new situations and pushes into the anxiety, she'll be working on resetting that alarm system. But there's a good chance—almost a guarantee—that her well-trained, hair-trigger amygdala will be set off. She can find security in some physical tools she can use as she practices; these skills can help her feel better equipped as she takes risks.

Ah, you might be saying to yourself, *they're finally getting to the relaxation part of treating anxiety. This is what I've heard about. This is what I was taught.*

Or you might be shaking your head in confusion. *Wait, is this about relaxing? Wilson and Lyons just told me over and over that the goal is be willing to get uncomfortable, and now they're going to talk about relaxing? Which is it? Be uncomfortable? Or be relaxed?*

Well . . . both. We want your child to be able to manage the body's reactions so the alarm system quiets down. When she steps into scary situations, she'll feel uncomfortable for a while. She will feel more *willing* to be uncomfortable if she believes that she can handle those uncomfortable sensations without losing control and making them worse. Children and their parents benefit greatly from understanding what the physical symptoms are all about. Knowing how the alarm system fires off—how it sends that blast of epinephrine through the body and activates those protective systems—takes away the mystery. Knowing how to step back and breathe a bit allows her to shift out of the danger mind-set.

Feeling uncomfortable is not the same as setting off your alarm system. But often, at the first sign of physical discomfort, anxious children begin to talk to themselves in a way that ramps up their fear. The amygdala, with its accompanying physical sensations, then responds accordingly. Now your child is not only afraid of the school play but is freaked out about her increased heart rate or jumpy tummy. Understanding what's happening, taking some nice calming breaths, loosening some muscles, and, of course, talking to herself differently . . . these all slow down the alarm system. In a nutshell, your child takes control back by being able to say, "Yep, there's that anxious tummy again. I get what's happening. Let me take a few moments to regroup. I can slow down my body so that I can shift my thinking back to where it needs to be."

The message is not that we are trying to eliminate the physical symptoms but that we can perceive them through a different lens. You may recall the story of golfer Webb Simpson (see Chapter 4), who experienced uncomfortable physical sensations as he stepped up to sink the winning putt at the U.S. Open golf tournament. He understood why the sensations were arriving at that moment. He didn't stop his play to stop his hands from shaking and get the feeling back in his numb legs. He accepted them and played *through* them.

Try this: Stop reading for a moment and take a slow, easy breath through your nose. Relax your facial muscles as you exhale. (We'll wait.) Now take that slow, easy breath through your nose one more time. Now sit quietly for another few moments as you let yourself breathe normally. Notice how you feel now. That's just the kind of small break we are talking about. (Continue reading when you're ready.)

Dealing with the Physical

Children often believe the physical symptom *is* the problem. "I can't go to school because I have a headache," or "I won't ride the bus because my stomach hurts." When making a trip to the nurse's office, they don't complain of anxiety or stress but of a physical symptom that they can't tolerate. How often do kids say, "Please call my parents to pick me up. My anxiety is triggering some somatic symptoms"? Not too often.

Adults are no different. In a recent study, almost 40 percent of patients referred by their doctor to a cardiac outpatient unit for evaluation were suffering from a psychological, not physical, condition. None suffered from arrhythmias that required treatment, and only 4 percent were diagnosed with coronary artery disease. Similar results are found for gastrointestinal issues, headaches, and hives.

One child who started treatment with us wore newly prescribed eyeglasses. Though acutely anxious when he arrived, he was a great student of the skills we teach and finished up his sessions after a few months. He returned a year or so later for a little tune-up—without his glasses. "When we went back to the eye doctor for his checkup, his eyes were absolutely perfect," his mom said. "The eye doctor believes the trouble with his vision was a temporary thing based on his stress last year."

It's important to remember that physical sensations, even when caused by anxiety, are *physical*. People are often offended when they're told after a trip to the emergency room with chest pain that it's stress related. They interpret the doctor's evaluation as "You're faking" or "There's nothing wrong with you." Our culture doesn't respond as sympathetically to anxiety symptoms as it does to physical illness. Some people would rather be told they're having heart issues than anxiety problems because they feel less ashamed about it. They don't perceive the implied message of "It's all in your head" as validating or compassionate. When we tell our children that they're "not really sick," they feel like we don't understand the discomfort and fear they're trying to manage.

The message to convey instead? "There *is* something wrong! Your alarm system is getting so fired up that the body is responding physically, absolutely creating a problem. But let's look at the source of all this trouble and address the relationship between your thoughts and your body."

When a child vomits on the first day of school, the vomit is not imaginary vomit. Migraines brought on by stress and anxiety are just as painful. If you've ever blushed from embarrassment, your face was truly red and blotchy and warm. Let's acknowledge the power of our children's anxious thinking. Truly, it's impressive. But the symptoms are the end result of a predictable pattern, and if we can change the pattern, we can influence the symptoms.

As therapists, we also don't want to mistakenly assume that the symptoms are anxiety related, so we're happy when children first see us after being evaluated by their physician. Many parents schedule an initial appointment with us because the medical tests for stomach issues or other symptoms came back negative, showing no problem. Even though the parents suspected anxiety was the culprit all along, they want to be sure they're not missing anything, which is wise.

After your child has been physically cleared and you know you're dealing with anxiety, we encourage you not to take the child back to the doctor solely for reassurances. Such appointments become a crutch, as we talked about in Chapters 5 and 6.

One boy we knew had ongoing stomach complaints and a fear of vomiting. (You've probably figured out by now that with anxious kids this fear is common.) After several medical appointments and tests, all negative, he still refused to go to school unless his mom called the doctor's office and had the doctor or nurse reassure him that he was okay. Some days he required an actual medical visit. His parents did what he asked because they wanted him to get to school, but he learned nothing about how his anxiety was causing his distress. His belief in his "illness" grew stronger by the day. Another parent, a pediatric nurse herself, understood on one level that her son had anxiety, but remained so worried about the possibility of a medical condition that she routinely took her son to her workplace health center for evaluation "just to be sure."

Parents often ask us about the use of over-the-counter medications to deal with physical symptoms, such as Tums for a tummy ache. Many parents find that placebos—fake treatments that the patient believes are going to be effective—work well, too (which doesn't surprise us at all), so they give gummy bears for headaches or baby aspirin as a sleep aid. Like a kiss on a boo-boo, the child gets the message, "I'm going to be okay." When it comes to the physical symptoms of anxiety, this is what the worried child wants to hear, so the symptoms actually lessen simply based on the child's belief that they should lessen.

Placebos work. In fact, in research conducted at Harvard Medical School, adults with irritable bowel syndrome (IBS) who were told they were taking a placebo improved as much as those on the very best IBS medications.

Are placebos a problem when dealing with your anxious child? Maybe. But we believe that your child should learn to use his own resources to manage anxiety rather than consistently seeking out external reassurance and comfort.

For example, Bobby is anxious about going to school on the bus, fearful that he will throw up. Mom gives him a pill that will stop this from happening. It works! Bobby doesn't throw up. But how did he get that outcome? He told himself that he wouldn't be sick because of the pill Mom gave him. He reacted differently as he got on the bus and played with his friends. "I don't need to worry about vomiting because the pill I took prevents that from happening." The pill gets all the credit. If we want our kids to learn to manage anxious situations, we should not promote this message.

Why? Because treating only the symptoms, without addressing the thought patterns and beliefs that fire off those body reactions, is like putting a bucket under the drips of a leaky ceiling without ever climbing up to repair the leaky roof. Having had leaky roofs more than once, we know that a bucket comes in quite handy while we fix the problem. But if we never invest in fixing the roof, we have to continually empty that bucket.

The next piece of the puzzle, BREATHE!, is the part of the plan designed to give you and your child an opportunity to pause, reboot, and get back on track. It's the bucket catching the water while you figure out how to repair the roof. Instead of a fake pill or magic potion that comes from the outside, a breathing skill is internal. In its own small way it is building your child's independence. But keep this in mind: Relaxing by itself is not the treatment. It's one possible component of a package deal.

By helping your child understand why the symptoms show up and how to respond to them differently, you begin to shape a different plan for your family. If incorporating a new breathing skill helps your child to manage his distress, then this piece of the puzzle will increase your child's sense of mastery and autonomy.

We're going to review two simple deep breathing skills that we call Calming Breath and Calming Counts. In Chapter 11 we help you pass these skills on to your children. For now we focus on helping you master them, with instructions for practice in the Time to Take Action section at the end of this chapter.

We promise that when you need them, these breathing skills can serve as handy ways to reset your body and your mind. As you and your child work through the puzzle pieces, your frustration may mount, your temper could flare, and your patience might run thin. The more often you practice these breathing reboots, the more access you'll have to your own rational, consistent parenting responses. There's just no down side to breathing calmly: we should all do it more often!

Calming Breath takes only thirty seconds, but you'll be surprised how it can quiet you if you devote your full attention to this half minute of refreshment. Begin by exhaling all the way. Then take a nice gentle breath in until you fill your lungs. Then exhale slowly and subvocalize a word or phrase that reminds you to quiet down, like "calm" or "relax" or "let go." Let your body and mind respond to that invitation. Then simply hang out for the next ten or fifteen seconds, remaining as mentally quiet as possible.

When a bit more time and focus are needed to calm physical tension and racing thoughts, turn to Calming Counts, which takes about ninety seconds. During that minute and a half, you have to concentrate on all the steps of the skill, because when concentrating in this manner, the brain can't also be worrying. For Calming Counts, follow the same instructions as with Calming Breath. But at the end of that long exhale, simply observe your next ten breaths without doing anything to control your breathing. Count each exhale in your mind, beginning with 10, descending to 1. Be as mentally quiet as possible during that time, focusing only on the task at hand.

Calming Breath and Calming Counts can help in two ways. First, you have a chance to feel more physically relaxed. Second, by following the instructions you pull your attention away from any not-so-helpful worried or stressed-out thoughts. Then, once calmed down a little, you can more easily say, "Those thoughts aren't helpful. I'm letting them go." That's what we're looking for: a reset of your mind and body.

NORMAL NERVOUSNESS AND
ANXIETY SENSITIVITY

There is another significant reason to master skills that calm your body and mind: you or others in your family may have a built-in tendency to be intolerant of anxiety. If that's true, we suggest that you also consider adopting two seemingly contradictory stances: accept the fact that you might be sensitive, and simultaneously practice reducing your sensitivity.

Have you noticed how some people seem better able than others to handle stress? We may classify certain folks as "adrenaline junkies" and others as having a "delicate nature." Another way to think of it: some people have the nervous system of a racehorse, while others have the nervous system of a turtle. Emergency room doctors and paramedics confirm that while one subgroup of patients is terrified by the slightest twinge of pain or discomfort, others walk around with all the signs of a heart attack but won't pay any attention until they fall over.

This difference intrigued researchers as well. In 1985 Richard McNally and Steven Reiss proposed the idea of "anxiety sensitivity," which refers to how people interpret and respond to the sensations of stress or anxiety, such as an increased heart rate, shakiness, butterflies in the stomach, and so on. McNally and Reiss determined that people with low anxiety sensitivity can handle a great deal of stress and interpret what's happening in their bodies as normal and expected reactions. In contrast, people with high anxiety sensitivity cannot handle much stress at all. They believe that stress is harmful, and they fear any stress-related sensations. They interpret even minor sensations as a sign of something catastrophic, like a heart attack or a nervous breakdown. Steven Reiss later wrote, "If you want to know who will have trouble coping with stress, it is more important to know what the person thinks will happen to him or her as a consequence of experiencing stress than to know how much stress the person experiences." Sound familiar?

If you have high anxiety sensitivity, you can react fearfully to what might be normal sensations. You now understand that if you interpret something as dangerous, your amygdala secretes epinephrine and you then experience even more intense sensations. Research has shown that high anxiety sensitivity is a predictor of anxiety and panic attacks, as well as a low tolerance for pain. If your child doesn't know how to interpret bodily sensations and overreacts to normal nervousness, then he will likely perfect the not-so-helpful skill of jumping to catastrophic conclusions and juicing up his alarm system. Let's keep helping your child grow up to be a low-anxiety-sensitivity adult.

We do a lot of public speaking, and both of us enjoy it. Some people think we're crazy because our motto could easily be "the bigger the audience, the better." Does that mean we don't get nervous? Heck no. We want to do well, and it's a bit risky to stand up in front of hundreds of people who may or may not agree with what we have to say. What if someone asks a question we can't answer? What if some people get up and walk out?

Moist hands, not much of an appetite, quickened heart rate, some worry thoughts popping up—we know this is going to happen. We actually expect it. It lessens after we teach a new workshop several times, but it's always there to some degree. Neither of us have high anxiety sensitivity, but we put ourselves in high-challenge situations. Nervousness comes with the territory. As you and your child put yourselves in your challenging situations, you should expect certain anxious sensations to show up with your worried thoughts, too.

We asked our friend Dante, an amateur but very skilled bicycle racer, what he feels like on the starting line of a race. His exact words: "Good. A little anxious, but it's fine." Dante shakes out his arms and legs before he gets on the bike, breathes, and waits for the starting gun. Once he pedals a few hundred feet, he's set. We can relate. As we begin a workshop, we take a few calming breaths, and once we get rolling we're fine. Those sensations are there, but they are not our focal point.

Research shows that anxiety sensitivity is a malleable trait. It can change! How can you help members of your family change? We'll give you some suggestions in Time to Take Action at the end of the chapter, but here are two important contributions. First, convey to your family the fact that some people are simply built to be more sensitive to anxious sensations. Take the mystery out of your tendencies to overreact. Second, *normalize* the body's reactions, even the unpleasant ones. As each of you learns to expect and tolerate these sensations, your amygdala will stop making you anxious about feeling anxious. The key messages that reflect this change are:

- I understand what my body is doing.
- I can handle what my body does.
- I can tolerate discomfort.

TIME TO TAKE ACTION:
Applying the Concepts of Chapter 8

Just for Parents

1. What are you or other family members role modeling and saying about nervousness in the body? How can you shift the way everyone reacts to the arrival of anxiety, including its physical calling cards?

2. Take a moment to think about how your family (current and your family of origin) handles and talks about physical symptoms and illness.

   • Are you fearful of your child's or your own physical symptoms?

   • What message do you give your child about illness, wellness, and physical symptoms? What messages did you as a child get from your parents or caregivers?

   • Do any of your close relatives suffer from physical symptoms that are attributed in the family to nerves? How about family members and relatives in the past?

   • If you had a conversation with your pediatrician about how your family approaches illness or physical symptoms, what can you imagine the doctor would say (if completely truthful)?

3. Take time to practice the Calming Breath and Calming Counts skills. Practice them frequently in the beginning so that your body and mind learn to work together in the process. The skills should be well-rehearsed, ready to go when needed.

Your goal should be to repeat the practices often enough so that spontaneously throughout the day you remind yourself, *This seems like a good time to take a little break and regroup.* It's best to master the skills when you are not feeling anxious. Then aim to stop for one of these mini-breaks about six times a day. Look for times of transition, such as when you are waiting at a traffic light, after working intensely on a project, just after you finish a phone call, right before you step into a meeting, and, of course, whenever you find yourself struggling with your children.

Calming Breath

1. Breathe out all the way.
2. Take a deep breath in, letting your belly expand first, and then your chest.
3. Slowly exhale, saying "calm" or a similar word under your breath. (We like "okay," or sometimes "fine." Keep it simple.)
4. Let your muscles go limp and warm; loosen your face and jaw muscles.
5. Remain in this "resting" position for a few more seconds, without thinking about your breathing or anything else.

Calming Counts

1. Breathe out all the way.
2. Take a deep breath in, letting your belly expand first, and then your chest.
3. Slowly exhale, saying "calm" or some other simple word under your breath.
4. Now take ten gentle, easy breaths, while you silently count down with each exhale, starting with 10 on the first exhale, 9 on the second exhale, and so on.
5. At the same time, invite the muscles in your jaw or forehead or stomach to loosen. Imagine them loosening.
6. Simply focus on taking these ten easy, loose, gentle breaths that give a calming message to your entire body and brain. While counting down and getting loose, feel free to smile. Breathe. Loosen. Smile.

Model the Process . . .
of Using Breathing as a Way to Pause and Reset

1. In front of your child, take a breath and pause as you move into something challenging. Explain what you're doing with messages like, "Boy, this is complicated. Let me just breathe and think for a moment." Or while driving, at a red light, announce that you're taking a few calming breaths so that you can handle the frustration of traffic and lousy drivers.
2. Talk to your children about stress-related symptoms and what you're doing to manage them. If you're doing nothing, think about starting something!

3. Share your little successes out loud. How did you use your breath to regroup? Did it work? What was easier after you took a few calming breaths? "I went to visit Aunt Phoebe at the nursing home yesterday. Before I went in I sat in the parking lot and took ten calm breaths. She can be so demanding, but it helped me to be in a calmer mindset going in!"

Stepping Toward the Bigger Picture

What's currently on your to-do list? Pick up groceries. Change the time of that dentist appointment next month. Buy a birthday card for your sister. Okay, what about the bigger tasks? You know what we mean: the stuff that's been sitting on the list for a while now. Reorganize the files in your office. Repair that ugly brown spot in the ceiling where it leaked three winters ago. Return the call from your insurance agent who wants to talk about some additional life insurance.

You'll feel great after you accomplish any of these tasks. Doing them, however, is less than inspiring. They involve time and steps and a certain amount of discomfort. So you put them off. We know how it goes. You just don't feel like it.

When it comes to kids and worry, not *feeling* like trying a new or difficult activity creates a major hurdle. How many times have you heard your child say something like, "It's okay. I decided I don't want to go to the party that much anyway," or "I don't really feel like trying out for the soccer team anymore." You sense that your child truly does want to participate, but the worried feelings stop him from moving forward. Worry convinces him it's not worth the inevitable, uncomfortable struggle.

The next piece of the puzzle, KNOW WHAT YOU WANT, explains how kids can move through this predictable obstacle. After all, the tools we've provided thus far must be put into action. You and your child need a way to push into new territory, which requires a clear picture of the outcome your child wants. Without an important goal or desire, what kid would want to take on the difficult feelings that go along with the new strategies we've been describing?

Asking children to step into worry can be a hard sell, but it's vital they take such action because worry *must* be present in order for them to learn a new way to manage it. We can increase their motivation to take the risk of facing those worries if we help children pick goals that they really want to accomplish. Having a desirable goal truly makes tackling worry easier. That sounds rather obvious, doesn't it? But for anxious kids and teens, the fearful event that is directly in front of them causes them to turn away from their original goal. We need to help them focus some of their attention on what good outcomes might be on the other side of their struggle with fear.

In this chapter we explain the skills that help anxious children find and focus on that goal without worry interfering and then calling the shots. The steps to reach a goal may not be easy, but when kids *want* to reach the goal, their minds then focus on making it happen rather than on avoidant escape.

GOTTA GET A WANT-TO

Let's go back to that to-do list for a moment. Call to mind an item on your life's to-do list that you have already accomplished. Something big. Significant. A success that even now, as you remember it, fills you with unmistakable satisfaction. Got it? Okay, now think about what you had to do to make it happen—the many steps, the setbacks, the days you didn't think it would happen, the stuff you endured that was irritating or even frightening. But you kept going. Why? Because you wanted it badly enough to tolerate the uncomfortable steps it took to get there.

Thus, as you put these tools into action, you must help your child find a goal that is truly important to her. In Chapter 12, we give you a framework to identify a goal, create a plan to get there, and then coach your child through the actual process. In the meantime, you can begin to talk together about what she wants to accomplish. What does she wish she could do? In what activities does she long to participate? One of our adult clients finally got on a plane to Disney World (and used the tools she'd been hesitant to practice) when her husband announced that if she wanted to make the two-day drive, she could. He and the kids would fly two hours and enjoy the first two days of the family vacation at the park, not on the interstate. Without her. Her worries about flying no longer felt insurmountable when she imagined her family having fun while she drove. Knowing what outcome you want and really wanting that outcome can motivate you to face what you fear.

Anxious children are quick to deny and push away their desires as a means of managing their worries. For many kids, it's just too disappointing and painful to want an outcome but then allow their worries to convince them it's not possible. Instead of wishing they could attend overnight camp or participate in the school musical, it's as if they make a deal with themselves and their worry: "I'll just stop wanting this stuff, and then I won't have to feel bad anymore about what I'm missing." It's easier in the short run to accept worry's control and choose to step back from life. We understand this stance, because without any effective strategies to handle worry, children protect themselves from more hurt. Avoidance, once again, is reinforced. When they come up against fear or uncertainty, they stop. *If I have to feel like* this *to get to* that, they tell themselves, *then why bother?*

This pattern of resignation is a type of emotional armor, so be prepared for some resistance to changing it. Moving out into the world, with all of its bumps and bruises, feels risky. Worried kids are more comfortable staying away from all that anguish. American author James Baldwin wrote, "Nothing is more desirable than to be released from an affliction, but nothing is more frightening than to be divested of a crutch."

Denying what you want—and accepting anxiety's demands to stay stuck—is an emotional crutch that needs to change. When we help children acknowledge that they truly want an outcome—and that anxiety is in the way—we begin to challenge passivity and negativity, two of anxiety's powerful henchmen.

Perhaps you've been minimizing the costs of worried avoidance in an effort to keep your child comfortable. "It's fine if you don't go to the party. We'll do something even more fun at home." Or "Lots of people never fly in airplanes. Who cares?" But here is the new message to offer your child: "It's okay—and actually helpful—to talk about what you want and to be open about how worry has gotten in the way of that." If he chooses to pursue a meaningful goal, will some disappointments occur along the way? Certainly. This process takes practice, but having a want-to energizes you both for the hard work ahead.

How do you help your child identify and begin to invest energy into the goals he's been pushing aside? Talk to him about his interests, what he wishes he could do, or what he might be missing. Ask a question such as, "If your worry had no power over you, what would you want to do? Where can you imagine going? What activity sounds fun to you?" As you engage in these exploratory conversations, your child may spontaneously verbalize his internal struggle between *wanting* to participate in an activity and *not wanting* to feel afraid and insecure along the way. One mother told us about her daughter Frannie, who talked routinely about her "wish" that she could learn to ride a horse but refused to try it because "she didn't know what might happen." Another boy quit soccer because he worried about his unfamiliar new coach "being mean," but talked about how much he missed playing with buddies and how he wished he could "know about his coach ahead of time."

We parents also need our children to cooperate with certain expectations: attending school, sleeping in their own beds, taking the bus because we can't be late for work, or coming home to a babysitter. Parents sometimes say to us, "I need her to [fill in the blank], but she's happy leaving it the way it is." In this case, frame your need as a *family* goal, one that is important to address because putting anxiety in charge is not working for several members of the family.

A family-oriented goal for a child might sound like, "I'm willing to ride the bus because I know Mom needs to get to work on time," or "I'll sleep in my own bed because no one in the family is getting enough sleep." This approach is not about making your child feel guilty or responsible for your needs. But anxious children—especially as they move into adolescence—can be overly focused on their own feelings and demands, not realizing that anxiety has a negative impact on relationships and social development. Figuratively (and sometimes literally) we need to teach our children to lift up their heads and look around at worry's ripple effect on the family. Help foster the skills of connecting rather than isolating, and becoming more flexible and compromising with others rather than taking rigid stands.

Taking It One Scary Step at a Time

Let's assume that you and your child have identified a want-to, a picture of where he hopes to go. He can say with conviction that he *does* want to go on the class trip or to stay home alone after school for an hour until you arrive from work. But the likelihood of doing what it takes to make that actually happen? You both wonder how far he'll get in making that intention a reality. Many steps take place along the way, and each is a potential deal breaker, an anxiety-laden barricade. What to do?

With the help of a motivating goal, children can adopt a new mindset. As they engage in each step along the way, they can *choose* to feel uncomfortable. They can *decide* to tolerate the doubt and distress that will inevitably show up. They can *want* the experiences that they don't like. Sound contradictory? Paradoxical? You're right, but there is method behind our madness.

Worries are going to show up as we try new activities. We do not have to get rid of them, but we do have to manage them. How? When we experiment with new behavior, we manage our worries by being willing to *not know* how well we will perform. We also have to trust that we can cope with the different possible outcomes. We need to know what we want and feel determined to get it. Then we need to be willing to put up with some hard times and some uncertainty, because the potential benefit is worth the risk.

But remember that merely tolerating discomfort and getting through it, like white-knuckling it across the bridge in Chapter 6, can be too soft of an approach. To really be a player in the game of life, we can't just put up with discomfort, we need to *embrace* it. We say to ourselves, "I am so motivated to do this that I *welcome* the discomfort that comes along with it." This powerful paradoxical strategy is a big challenge to your child's point of view and probably to yours as well. But we are simply building on the ideas of the earlier puzzle pieces. Worry is a natural part of learning and growing; we are going to expect it, move toward it, and even *voluntarily accept it* because it's an inevitable part of going after what we want in life.

Marissa's story illustrates how this paradoxical stance takes form in real life. Marissa, a forty-two-year-old mother of three, wants to lose some weight, in large part due to a family history of heart disease. She's very clear about this want-to, but also nervous because she's tried and failed many times before. She's aware of the gap that exists between her desire to lose weight and her lack of enthusiasm for the uncomfortable steps she must take in order to get there. For example, her mother is a fabulous baker and loves to bring over goodies for her family. Of course, having cookies and brownies in the house all the time makes it hard for Marissa to stick to her plan. She wants to tell her mom to lay off the yummy deliveries. They live only a block from each other, so the kids can visit Grandma's when they want a treat. But telling her mother what she needs makes Marissa uncomfortable and anxious. "I want to lose the weight, but the idea of hurting my mother's feelings . . . and then having *another* conversation with her about my weight. . . . I'm afraid. I just don't know if I can *do* that."

Marissa will have a harder time losing weight until she embraces the discomfort of this conversation with her mother, which is merely one of many challenging steps she must take to reach her goal. Success requires her to think, *I want to lose weight. It's important to me. Having this conversation with my mother might scare me, but I am going to see it as a part of my goal. I want to lose weight, so I am willing to tell my mom, "No more treats at the house."*

No matter what anxious people are afraid of or what they want, welcoming the fear of new and challenging experiences helps keep them moving. Marissa needs to view her discomfort with her mother as an expected part of the experience. If she is going to eventually feel comfortable setting limits with her mother, then she must start by having an uncomfortable conversation. To achieve her goal of protecting her health, Marissa can't avoid this challenge or any of the other uncomfortable steps she must take, like joining a gym and exercising in front of other people. If she does take the steps, she makes each of them easier to tolerate if she welcomes them as part of the process.

Why would she take such a crazy stance? Because it is the most pragmatic attitude during these uncertain moments. When you resist feeling afraid, fear sticks around. When you allow it, when you fully experience it—when you *welcome* it—you remove a complete layer of fear. You stop being afraid of being afraid. You stop worrying about being uncomfortable.

Although this logic is simple, it is also novel. We suspect that you and your child are like most everybody else in the world: you have never approached worry this way. Here's what you need to remember: choosing a difficult experience makes that experience less painful.

We reach our goals by taking each step along the way. We have two choices as we face any next step. We can want to take it, or we can fight and resist taking it. If you attempt a new and threatening activity and simultaneously resist it, you send conflicting messages to your brain. It's like pressing the gas and brake pedals of your car at the same time. Lots of noise, not much progress.

> Stop reading and take a moment to visualize this: see yourself trying to physically take a step forward as you simultaneously fight and resist moving your legs. If you need help experiencing that picture, see a giant rubber band looped around your ankles. As soon as you attempt to extend one leg, feel the band immediately tighten. How quickly would you exhaust yourself as you take steps toward your goal?

The brain needs one consistent message, and then it will line up your body and mind to match that message. All of us make much greater strides when we stop resisting and actually become willing to experience even the difficult steps that are inevitable along the way to our desired goals.

The strategy is to turn a *have-to* into a *want-to*.

Choose Fewer Battles

If you've ever moved, we doubt you really felt like packing the dishes into boxes. Or calling the utility companies. Or sending out change-of-address cards. But you did these chores because you wanted to complete your move. In your imagination, you let yourself see your new home and reminded yourself of how good it would eventually feel to be done.

You've already achieved a number of important goals in your life. The routes that you took were full of challenging obstacles, including difficult feelings, struggles, anguish, and uncertainties. But you kept going, moving through the tough times, with your focus on what you wanted. You didn't let those feelings take charge, but you couldn't completely banish them either. Instead, you looked for ways to push forward whether you were comfortable or not. In order to get to the big finish, you had to embrace the tough steps on the path.

Anxious kids don't like those steps along the way. As soon as they hit discomfort or uncertainty, they retreat. They're quick to decide it's too hard. Your task is to convince them that the steps are a part of the process, and a willingness to move through the steps and be uncomfortable is the quickest way to get to the goal.

Let's go back to Marissa. In order to meet her goal, she has to have that tough talk with her mom. She has to exercise, too, which means changing around her family's schedule, asking her husband for help, and getting up earlier. She decides to get an app on her phone to track her food, which takes time and focus. She must change the foods she buys at the grocery store and stop drinking soda at work.

This is not easy, and Marissa can make it much harder by pressing her proverbial gas pedal and brake at the same time. She has a goal that's important to her, but if she resists each step along the way, she sounds like this:

- "I want to lose weight, but I'm not going to talk to my mom. I'll just stay away from the treats."
- "I hate to exercise in the morning. Ugh. It's so painful to get up. And I'm so embarrassed for people in the aerobics class to see me."
- "It's not fair that I have to watch everything I eat when other people can eat whatever they want."
- "I hate drinking water. I miss my soda. This stinks."

Here's an alternative stance. Marissa wants to lose weight so that she can feel healthier, so she embraces the steps to get her there, recognizing the challenges but focusing on her goal. She sounds like this:

- "I want to lose weight, and so I will talk to my mom. My goal is worth tolerating her getting annoyed with me. I'm scared, but I can handle it."
- "I want to exercise because it will get me to my goal quicker. I've never liked getting up early, but I'm going to try some new classes. I'll probably feel like an idiot at first, but I'll push through that."
- "Tracking what I eat is part of my plan. I'll do it because I'm committed to my plan."
- "I want to drink more water if that will help me reach my goal."

Once Marissa stops fighting the steps and becomes totally committed to her project of feeling healthier, she gives her brain one consistent message instead of two conflicting ones. Does she start to love exercise? Not at first, but she gets there, feeling great after every workout. Does she still crave soda at times? Want cake? Have to listen to her kids complain about the lack of junk food in the house?

Absolutely. If she could protect herself from heart disease without changing any of her former habits, she gladly would have done so. But she wants to achieve her goal, so she must turn the have-tos into want-tos.

Think about Frannie, the girl who wished to ride a horse. In order to reach this outcome, she will face a lot of have-tos along the way. If she were making a list, she might write:

- I have to step toward my fear of the unknown.
- I have to sign up for lessons.
- I have to tolerate feeling nervous as I sit in the saddle for the first time.
- I have to feel small and tall at the same time while I'm sitting on a big horse.

These are simply the facts; she *will* have to engage in these steps. But if she *talks* to herself in *have-to* terms, she won't feel very motivated. It's best if she talks to herself in *want-to* terms. "I want to be a part of the next round of lessons, so I'm going to sign up this week. I know I'll be afraid in the beginning, but it will be worth it in the end. I'd like to get that tough part over with: to just sit there in the saddle that first time and let myself feel nervous. I'm sure I'm going to feel pretty small on that big horse. At the same time, I'll be sitting about five feet up in the air. That will be a little unnerving, but I can do it. I look forward to how I'm going to feel after a few lessons."

When you introduce this idea to your child, you'll talk about the successes you've both had and your willingness to take the steps you needed to get there. (At the end of this chapter, in Time to Take Action, we give you some additional guidance.) Play around with this idea, too: The more we resist the steps—complaining, avoiding, moaning, and whining—the longer it takes to reach the goal. The more willing we are to move into the steps, the quicker we get what we want.

Our stance might be sounding crazy to you about now. Maybe offering these examples to your children can help illustrate our logic:

- You want to make the team, but you refuse to practice before try-outs.
- You want money to buy new skis, but you won't do your chores.
- You want to make pizza at home tonight, but you're unwilling to go back out to buy the ingredients.
- You'd like to start dating, but you can't tolerate getting rejected.

Anxious children are used to avoiding; they focus their attention and energy on getting out of situations. You're likely familiar with how they fight against each step. We know that if they practice *wanting* to take each step—and are willing to take the risk—they learn to move more quickly and efficiently without all the wasted energy of fighting back, resisting, analyzing or negotiating. When kids allow themselves to look forward to reaching a goal, and then willingly take each of the steps needed, then the steps and the process become easier.

What happens, though, when kids are afraid to take the steps, when they don't believe they can handle those steps? Frannie may truly want to learn to ride a horse, but she just doesn't think she can sit up there and not fall off. Your teenage son may really want to go to the prom, but taking the step of asking a girl in his science class—and having her say no—is too risky. In his mind, he imagines the failure and humiliation.

A simple, logical formula helps illustrate the stance that you and your child must practice and embrace:

> **"Since I want [desired outcome],**
> **then I'm willing to [take this less-than-desirable step]**
> **to get there."**

Find examples to begin using this point of view with your child. You don't have to tackle the anxiety-ridden content; just help your family get used to the concept. Start with some obvious examples, stuff that everyone already does:

- I want to have fresh breath, so I'm willing to brush my teeth in the morning before I leave the house.
- I want to go to school without bed-head, so I'll brush my hair, too.
- I want to walk upright today rather than fall on my face, so I'm going to keep my shoelaces tied in double knots.

For yourself, you can then move into more challenging or adult issues that require some definite effort:

- I want to get the house painted this summer, so I'm willing to look at the budget and see where I can cut back on expenses this winter.
- I want to have my Sunday free, so I'm willing to get all the errands done on Saturday.
- I want to move to a bigger house, so I'm willing to meet with the bank about a larger mortgage.
- I want to see that movie on opening day, so I'm willing to plan ahead and buy tickets online.

When children apply this want-to attitude to the issues they struggle with, they fight less and participate more. They are rewarded with more energy to handle the expected discomfort that shows up when they face their fears, and they are better able to focus on problem solving. Momentum continues to build in the right direction as successes start to add up.

Except for one small problem.

Worry doesn't give up easily. It routinely inflicts amnesia on children in a way that seems to erase the wonderful gains they've made. This problem frustrates parents, to put it mildly. The next chapter addresses the problem of forgetting, and how supporting autonomy and problem solving in children is the bridge that connects them back to their successes.

TIME TO TAKE ACTION:
Applying the Concepts of Chapter 9

Just for Parents

1. The best way for you to convey this new logic of turning a have-to into a want-to is to *start working on yourself*. Notice how you approach the challenges in front of you, how you talk to yourself about the steps that stand between you and your goal. What are you showing your children? How can you demonstrate the process of stepping forward, even when it's uncertain and uncomfortable?

2. And how are you letting anxiety rule you and your family? Parents are often so anxious about their anxious child that they lose sight of how the whole family has been accommodating

worry. Think about and make a list of goals you may have for your family that anxiety seems to have interrupted. Are there activities that you know are good for your family but you have been unwilling to pursue because of your own worry or your reluctance to address your child's anxiety? What are you avoiding? Perhaps you want your children to have a consistent bedtime that gives you some peaceful time in the evening. How about an adult weekend away with friends or your partner? Or even a dinner date? Would you like your teenager to get a job to help with his own expenses but are fearful he couldn't handle it? Are you skipping possible vacations or activities for fear of the unexpected? Take a hard look at how anxiety may also rule the routine of your family or your child's siblings, and how the goal of a more flexible family life may require a willingness to take challenging steps.

3. Anxious children and especially teens tend to overly focus on *their* needs and emotions. Anxious kids are controlling. Talking about family goals—and how the anxiety impacts many relationships—helps kids shift out of an emotionally driven focus on themselves. You may have avoided addressing this in order to protect your child from feeling guilty about the anxiety, but realistically helping both parents and kids see the impact of staying the same—including the social cost in families and friendships—is a powerful motivator. Spend some time talking to your child about your needs, the family's needs, and the needs of others around them. Ask yourself and ask your child: How does anxiety get in the way of our family's life?

Plant the Seeds . . .
of Moving Toward a Goal

At the start of the chapter, we asked you to recall a goal on your life's to-do list that you accomplished. Tell that story to your child. Include the steps you took, the setbacks, the moments when you didn't think you'd get there, and how you kept yourself going. Have you ever told your children how you saved up to buy your first car by mowing lawns for three summers? Or how you made it through college while you worked at the dry cleaners? Or how amazing it was to taste those first vegetables out of your garden, after all those weeks of weeding and waiting? See how often you can plant the seeds of this message: "The steps were difficult, and I often didn't feel like doing them or even think I could, but I kept going."

Model the Process . . .
of Moving Toward a Goal

1. Talk to your child about one of your own current goals. Big and small goals are part of everyday life, so show your child how you move through the steps as a part of *your* want-to. You can do this casually. Bring it up at dinner or talk out loud to yourself. But—and this is important—the task here is to share your *problem-solving plans, not your worries.* Model for your child how you put together a plan of action. Want to get out of the house by 7:30 AM because you have an important meeting at 8:00? How are you going to make that happen? Want to fly to Florida with your kids so you don't have to drive for three days? How do you plan to handle flying, knowing that you don't really like it? Want to remodel the bathroom, even though it's difficult to arrange all the subcontractors

and make all the decisions? How are you going to manage
the stress of that project? What are you willing to endure in
order to get what you want? Let your child in on the challenges
and frustrations of the many steps as well as the supportive
thoughts and actions that keep you going.

2. Be aware of your language as you talk about these challenges.
   Use expressions that reflect your positive spirit. How will
   you illustrate turning a have-to into a want-to? How will you
   represent to your child the attitude that makes a tough task
   easier? How can you convey the ways that you embrace each
   step along the way? Hint: Notice the difference between
   saying, "As soon as we get this part over with, we can get on
   to the next step," versus "Oh, this is agonizing! I feel like it'll
   never get done!"

When Amnesia Attacks

Forgetting generally isn't helpful. Keys. Appointments. People's names. Where you left the computer's power cord or your wallet. That's why Post-it Notes have sold millions. The inability to remember what you know and whom you love and what you've done before is a heartbreaking consequence of certain brain injuries and illnesses. We're not trying to be overly dramatic here, but how you connect to past experiences and what you learn from those events are vital to navigating successfully through school, careers, and relationships.

Most of us have known someone who makes the same mistake over and over. We shake our heads and think, *Did she learn* nothing *from those last four relationships/jobs/dogs/speeding tickets?* We wonder how she could possibly forget how terrible/sad/time-consuming circumstances became the last time, and how long/painful/costly the process was to fix it.

What does this have to do with anxiety? We've given you some proven tools and strategies to tackle worry. We want you to experiment with the tools, and we expect that your family will create new patterns of reacting and behaving. But we also know that worry has the ability to take all you learn and dismiss it without hesitation. It's time to tackle one of the most frustrating and powerful aspects of dealing with anxiety: Worry can make you forget.

People often use the term "starting over" to describe a new job, a move to another state, a different phase of a relationship, or even a change in attitude. In actuality, we're rarely beginning completely anew. Even when we explore novel activities, we don't really start from scratch. All of us have had many life lessons and learned a variety of skills that we apply to these situations. That's how we learn and grow: we incorporate new experiences into our repertoire of preexisting beliefs and skills. To master any task, we have to start out naïve, a little awkward, and somewhat clumsy. But our memories of past successes remind us that we have the potential to manage this undertaking. Our unconscious minds automatically access memories of past successes that we can apply to the new activity. That's how we allow ourselves to move toward a challenge instead of backing away from it. We think, *I've succeeded in similar experiences in the past. Those experiences reassure me that I have a chance to succeed at this one.* But when worry doesn't just show up but takes over, our self-doubt and insecurity block out those memories. In such circumstances we have to consciously work to retrieve our inner resources.

Worry disrupts this retrieval system by giving us amnesia. It gains ground by eliminating or minimizing what we've handled before, keeping our minds off those past successes and poking holes in our confidence. This next puzzle piece, BRIDGE BACK TO YOUR SUC-CESSES, helps challenge worry's amnesia by creating helpful "reminder bridges" that connect children back to their successes and enable them to build on their experiences.

Bridge Back
to Your
Successes

When worry dominates, we start to believe that we must know the specifics about unfamiliar or unique events. But success in new situations often depends not on knowing absolutes but on translating the skills we had *over there* to a related experience *over here*. New parents can feel overwhelmed, but recalling their experiences as a babysitter or taking care of younger siblings can help increase their confidence. You may have many questions about the specifics of a new job on your first day, but recalling how you learned the ropes, deciphered the politics, and earned promotions in previous jobs normalizes that discomfort. Perhaps you've never traveled to Asia, but your ability to manage glitches during other travel adventures gives you adequate confidence to step outside your comfort zone. Bridging back to memories of past successes, and even what we learned from past failures, helps us tolerate the uncertainty of unfamiliar experiences.

Anxious kids allow their worries to continue blaring in their heads without addressing how they might handle them. Their consciousness fills with worries, which then block their ability to remember past successes that might serve as current resources. Worried thoughts are a blanket signal to avoid.

Of course, all along we've been promoting a different tack: let's expect worries, normalize them, and create different responses. The response to focus on in this chapter? Use the *expected* arrival of worries (the puzzle piece of Chapter 4) as a cue to access past successes. Past successes become yet another source of internal encouragement to keep moving forward into the unknown.

In order for kids to generate reminder bridges, they must use their worries as triggers to remember past skills. Worries remind them that they might need to stop for a bit, regroup, back away, or problem solve. Then, once they've paused and regrouped, reminder bridges access the thoughts, ideas, and memories that kids can use and reuse as they face challenges.

Making these connections may not come naturally or automatically to children, especially when dealing with circumstances that, for whatever reason, heighten their worries. In fact, worried kids often outright deny ever having had a success. When eight-year-old Bethany refuses to go to her dentist appointment, her mother is baffled. "You've never had a problem at the dentist before. Even when you had that cavity filled last year, you were fine. I thought you liked Dr. Albee."

Bethany then seems to rewrite history: "I'm always scared when I go. I don't like it there. Remember when I cried the whole time?" Bethany's mom shakes her head. No, she doesn't remember a time when the dentist was even remotely an issue. She remembers plenty of other circumstances when a shy Bethany refused to participate in school activities or sleepovers, but never at the dentist. What's going on here? Bethany's anxiety is taking over new territory. Why the dentist? Hard to say. Maybe she saw something on television or a classmate told a story about getting teeth pulled. There might be no concrete explanation at all.

When faced with such a problem, we need to be mindful of that tricky content trap that tempts us to focus on changing the external environment ("Let's find a new dentist" or "I'll ask to sit with you during your cleaning") or find a "rational" explanation ("Did someone say something to you? Did something happen? Was Dr. Albee mean?")

Here's what we *do* know: Bethany's thinking has moved into "I can't handle it" mode. She's digging in her heels, plus she's unable to remember or acknowledge her past successes. She's stuck.

In order to model the strategy of constructing reminder bridges, start by showing your child that this is a natural process we all go through. Share examples from your own life. How have you managed an uncomfortable new situation by recalling a past success? In Chapter 4 we discussed the times in life when we can expect worry. Here's a reminder list to guide you:

- You're doing a new or different activity.
- You're unsure about your plans.
- You have a lot of "what if" questions.
- You have to perform.
- Something scary is happening.

Children benefit from hearing and watching what adults do well, so take that inside skill and model it. Let your child hear you build bridges. And if you haven't built them for yourself in the past, start! We want kids to know that when worry shows up, one of the helpful and routine patterns to practice looks like this:

Worry for a moment, then immediately bridge to my successes and move on.

Kids must internalize this skill by shifting how they talk to themselves. Bethany, disconnected from her positive visits to the dentist as well as her other successes, needs help talking to herself in a different, more historically accurate way. If we were helping Bethany with her newly blossomed dentist issue, we'd help her come up with these reminder bridges. Some deal with the dentist, but others reflect coping with any worry-provoking events.

Some of Bethany's Reminder Bridges

- "I've done fine at all my other dentist visits, so I'll probably do fine this time, too."
- "When new things happen at the dentist, I handle them, like my first cavity."
- "I usually feel worried when I'm starting something, but I get the hang of it quickly."
- "Even if I haven't handled this *exact* thing yet, I'm a good problem solver."
- "Every time I face a challenge, I remember my success during a past challenge."

With many of our clients, we create a worksheet like the one that follows. They can then see how they have already used this skill in their lives and how to apply it to other arenas. We want them to come to two important conclusions:

1. I have experience with this kind of event.
2. I think I can handle it.

I really want to . . .	That reminds me of how . . .	That reminds me how I can handle . . .
Go to that summer camp for a week.	I started sleeping over at Seth's house.	Being uncomfortable at first.
Jump off the high diving board.	I learned last summer to dive off the edge of the pool.	Feeling scared the first time I try something.
Try out for the school musical.	I got cut from the soccer team the first year, but made it the next year.	Not knowing if I'll make it, and even getting cut, too, if that happens.
Raise my hand and answer questions in class.	I answered everybody's questions about my project at the science fair.	Feeling nervous and doing it anyway.

Practicing Perfection

When any of us try a new activity—even when using skills from past successes—we're still taking a risk. Will it always turn out exactly as we want it to? No. Will it be uncomfortable? Maybe. Will we make mistakes as we learn? Yes, and we may even fail miserably. Anxious children often move away from such risks because they cannot tolerate frustration and mistakes. Past errors are not seen as necessary building blocks to learning but as unacceptable failures. You may have observed how this need for perfection shut down your child's willingness to grow and experiment.

As you shift away from offering reassurances of certainty, you may also have to address your anxious child's frequent need for everything to turn out just right. The idea of making a mistake is unbearable, and anxious children have no internal conversations about all they have learned already. Without bridges, they don't know how to remind themselves of what their past experiences illustrate: as you learn a new skill, you go through a brief period of feeling uncertain and uncomfortable. Mistakes are an inevitable part of mastering a skill.

When your child takes a stance of "I must do everything right the first time," she is holding on to an attitude that blocks progress. So we encourage you to add an important reminder message during this process: "Whenever you learn something new, expect that you're going to feel unsure, awkward, and maybe clumsy on your path to mastering it." An anxious child doesn't like to make mistakes, and she'll work hard to prevent them. She has likely enlisted your help to do it perfectly. Not anymore.

Anxious kids also have a difficult time believing that they can learn and change. As we've said, they lose their internal connection to the process of try, fail, adjust, try again, even though every child has moved through this process over and over again since babyhood. You can give your child a little quiz to bring home the point that he's quite capable of learning new skills, which is very different from offering the automatic external reassurance he might be expecting. We'll describe that quiz in the Time to Take Action section at the end of the chapter.

As kids start trusting their ability to manage difficulties, they can begin to feel more independent and more willing to take risks in lots of areas. Your actions will either help them or stifle their development. That's what we'll talk about next.

Autonomy Versus Anxiety: How a Child Stops Leaning and Starts Standing Up

When we don't like handling the tougher emotions such as anger and sadness, we tend to avoid dealing with conflict. If we are afraid that conflict will damage relationships—or is a sign of disrespect or is not how a "close" family acts—then we won't support open communication of different opinions. Although this tendency to avoid conflict is quite common, the latest research in child development shows us that it certainly has a negative impact on our children.

In contrast, when we teach our children how to express uncomfortable feelings and to work through conflict, we create a family environment in which kids are more willing to take on challenges. Couple that with the promotion of our children's problem-solving skills, and we are building an important foundation: the development of autonomy, which is more than simply preventing ourselves from overprotecting our kids. Our job as parents is to create an atmosphere that encourages our children to make decisions, develop their own opinions and views, and become self-reliant.

If you tend to accommodate your child's worries and avoidance, then you need to shift your style toward one that encourages her independence. There is a little bit of bad news here. For children to become autonomous—which every child *must* do to grow into a competent adult—they have to develop and express to the world their own unique opinion. Occasionally that opinion will be different from yours. In other words, one sign of good parenting is that your child openly argues logically with you. And—sometimes—she has to *win* those arguments. (Interpretation: That means sometimes you have to be a good sport about *losing* arguments.)

Mark Cummings, PhD, and other researchers at the University of Notre Dame study the interactions of children and their parents. Surprisingly, they have found that children's emotional well-being and sense of security are more affected by what they observe in the relationship *between* their parents than by how either parent interacts directly with the child. In one study, the children watched a video of a staged conflict between their parents. About halfway through the conflict, the researchers stopped the video. They then observed those children in a structured activity. One third of the kids acted aggressively, by shouting, getting mad, or punching a pillow.

Then the researchers made one small change. They allowed the children to observe the entire video, which concluded with their parents respectfully resolving the conflict. Again they observed the children in a structured activity. But this time only 4 percent acted aggressively. What's the takeaway message here? It's better than okay for your kids to observe you arguing. But it's important that you learn to openly and respectfully resolve those disagreements. Don't start fighting in front of your children and then withdraw into your bedroom to finish arguing in private (typically preceded by the admonishment, "Not in front of the children!").

All parents fight, and many have several disagreements a day. Dr. Cummings's research has shown that when children are exposed to constructive parental arguments that are resolved with affection, they develop a greater sense of security, learn how to compromise, and have better social interactions in school.

Then, of course, there are the disagreements you have directly with your child. Studies show us that how you manage your end of the argument is instrumental in your child's healthy development, especially as she becomes a teenager. It has less to do with how many arguments you have and more to do with the quality of those fights.

Psychologist Joseph Allen has been leading a research team on this topic at the University of Virginia, and their newest findings were published in 2012. Allen interviewed over 150 thirteen-year-olds about difficult arguments they've had with their parents. They returned to interview the same subjects when they turned fifteen and sixteen. One of their most important findings was that when parents seek to talk out problems with their teens and model how to discuss differences calmly, those kids carry these same positive lessons out into their peer community. By learning in the previous years that their parents respected their growing autonomy, they could use that trusted independent thinking to resist peer pressure. They were then *40 percent* more likely to say no when offered drugs or alcohol than kids who were not allowed to argue with their parents. The teens who felt intimidated to talk to their parents ended up being the ones more likely to acquiesce when offered drugs or alcohol.

We're not talking about allowing your child to yell at you, insult you, or simply whine and complain. But teaching your child the rewards of being calmly persuasive and giving your child confidence that you are approachable and will listen to her point of view—these parental tasks pay benefits for years to come. We get an added bonus here, too: When we teach our children that we will listen to their side of the story and take their point of view seriously, then our children will learn to listen to us as well. How do you begin this shift?

- Ask for your child's opinion.
- Show her that it's okay for her to express opinions that are different from yours. An insecure child will initially require your *permission* to express her differences and her sense of independence.
- Show respect for her point of view. Avoid judging or dismissing her opinions.

- Encourage her to take the risk of telling you what she wants or needs from *you*, so that she can eventually learn to do it with others. Insecure children are afraid that others will reject them if they assert themselves.
- Support other reasonable risks. Help her persist in the face of difficulties. Discourage her from escaping or avoiding. Remind her that getting out of her comfort zone is part of the strategy for gaining control.

The more you help her to think independently and convey her opinion openly to others, the more she will develop confidence in her problem-solving skills.

You're Getting Closer

You've made it to Chapter 10 and have moved through six of the seven puzzle pieces. Good work! We're hoping you've made some important shifts in the way you view worry. And if you haven't yet, we urge you to implement our suggestions within each chapter's Time to Take Action section. You won't be able to wait until Chapter 12 and then expect to coerce your child into facing what feels threatening to him. Finesse can work where coercion fails.

We also know that each step and each suggestion to change can be difficult for your child to accept. Anxious kids don't have much frustration tolerance. They are looking for a magic formula to eliminate their discomfort and struggles. You need to help your child accept that she won't automatically feel competent from the first time she uses a reminder bridge. She must repeat a pattern over and over before it begins to show up without a lot of conscious effort. And she certainly won't feel comfortable during those first few practices, so she has to be courageous. Help her practice her reminders when she's feeling worried. Praise her for offering herself the right message at the right time, while she simultaneously tolerates her worry and discomfort.

What do you need as the parent? You need faith and trust that your child can master these skills sufficiently to grow up to be a well-adjusted adult. You must stop protecting your child from all pain and injury, just like you had to risk her falling as a young toddler learning to walk. Keeping her 100 percent comfortable and safe now will handicap her in the future. Autonomy, remember?

Your child has likely learned to look to you to solve the difficulty or to make discomfort or uncertainty disappear. This is normal when children are young, but our job as parents is to move them from dependence toward independence. Allow her to experiment and move away from you. Let her get angry and frustrated as she figures out how to move through this challenge. Let her do the work.

Your child must learn how "talking to yourself" is a big part of that plan, and is the alternative to consistently seeking external guidance. Developing an internal message of "I can handle this" helps worry become just a momentary thought instead of a prediction of doom. Remember, worries come automatically for all of us. Our job is not to *remove* them. Our job is to have a response to manage the worry. Once we stop buying into their threatening content, worries will spontaneously fade over time.

TIME TO TAKE ACTION:
Practicing the Concepts of Chapter 10

You now have six pieces to this worry puzzle with only one piece to go. It's time for you to shift away from your role as provider of comfort and certainty and step into this big-picture framework of handling anxiety. We recognize that you might need some help changing your own automatic responses, the ones that seemed so effective for a time, but have not given your family a way to move out of worry. Here are several ideas to incorporate.

Just for Parents

1. Mentally review your child's daily routines. What are you doing for him that he can do for himself? Where can you support his autonomy? Find three opportunities for greater independence, but be prepared: relaxing your guard will probably make you feel a bit uncomfortable.

2. Ask for and listen to your child's opinions. She needs to be able to assert herself and express her ideas. When she disagrees with a rule or policy, encourage her to talk about what she wants to change or how she would go about solving the problem. Try bringing up a recurring conflict, or maybe she's already doing that for you. Start with one that feels manageable. "You've been complaining a lot about my boring cooking. Any ideas about how we might change the menu?" or "I think the no-hat policy in school makes sense. But I'd like to understand the reasons that you think it's stupid."

Plant the Seeds . . .
of Recalling and Using Past Successes

1. Kids love to hear positive stories about themselves, and we
   are the keepers of their histories. Talk to your child about a
   memory of her succeeding at a task, or talk to someone else
   about her while she is within earshot. "Oh, I saw a cardinal
   yesterday in the yard, and it reminded me of how *determined*
   Jenny was to set up that bird feeder when she was six. She
   was so worried the birds wouldn't show up, but by the middle
   of winter she had a daily flock visiting. Just remembering that
   makes me smile!" Does a photograph in the house capture
   some moment of family success? Someone holding a trophy?
   Standing proudly next to a just-completed snowman? Pick up
   that photo and say out loud (to no one in particular) something
   like, "Wow, that was such a moment! What a great memory."
   Plant the seeds of the message: "Recalling successes feels
   great and reminds us of how capable we are."

2. Give your child a playful little quiz about the skills he has
   developed over time. Have fun remembering tasks that he
   couldn't do when younger but now does without a thought.
   - How about physical competencies? Whistling? Tying shoes?
     Riding a bike? Can he recall when you took the training
     wheels off and he learned to balance on two wheels while he
     pedaled?
   - Think of any academic topics that were difficult for her to
     master but are now second nature. "How do you spell 'fulfill-
     ment' (or whatever tough words she currently knows how to
     spell)?" "What is three-fourths of one hundred?"

- What else do you know she has mastered? Ask if she has *always* been able to perform these tasks. The answer, of course, will be no.
- If there is a younger sibling, what can your child do that the sibling cannot yet do?
- Curiously inquire about the stages of skill development he passed through to accomplish that task. For instance, he learned about numbers, then moved to addition. Then subtraction. Then, a year later, he learned multiplication and division. Finally, he tackled fractions.

3. Bring home the point that your child does many activities easily now that were not easy at the start. Talk about the process that we all go through: from not knowing, to practicing or studying, and then to knowing; from unskilled, to awkward and clumsy, and then to skilled. Analyzing these examples illustrates to your child that she can tolerate the learning curve that comes before new skills come automatically. But she *will* learn, just like she learned to walk, to talk, to dress, and to feed herself. With practice. And more practice. And a bit of internal reassurance thrown in, too.

Model the Process . . .
of Talking Positively to Yourself—
Internal Reassurance

How do you talk to yourself? Are you encouraging? Critical? Do you step back from your stress to remind yourself of your strengths and your past successes? Do you build reminder bridges? If the answer is yes, then great! Now start doing it out loud, in front of your child. Share how you have created mental bridges to encourage yourself to move forward into new territories. Demonstrate how you talk to yourself when confronted with normal worries that show up at normal times.

If the answer is no, then here's your chance to change a pattern of your own while modeling this skill for your child. When young people hear that worry can be managed as a normal part of life's experiences, and when they observe the adults in their lives demonstrate that in a routine way, then they can treat worry differently when it arrives. Do you tend to say, "Oh, I am so stressed about this meeting! I can't eat breakfast. I always feel this way, and I hate it!"? Do you then hope that someone nearby will talk you down and give you reassurance? Try a new tactic that models a more supportive way to talk to yourself, one that connects you to your strengths and successes. "Well, I feel nervous before my big meeting today. This meeting is important to me, so I know worry will make an appearance. That's how it usually goes, but I know that once I get to the office and start talking, I'll handle myself just fine. I've done it so many times already." Make it a point to talk about how you expected and allowed worry to show up, then gave yourself a pep talk, remembered your successes, and got the job done.

11

Casey's Guide Will Help

You probably arrived at this point in the book from one of two directions. You may have read each chapter and then taken time to explore our suggestions within the corresponding Time to Take Action sections. You paused to reflect on your outlook about risk, safety, independence, and trust. You have begun to model new ways to respond to worry in your family, and you have discussed a variety of topics with your son or daughter to plant the seeds of change. Or perhaps you have been reading this book straight through, eager to learn what it takes to help your child become independent and courageous. If so, feel free to continue reading the entire book. Then return to the assignment of this chapter.

With the understandings you have gained from these first ten chapters, it's time to introduce your child to *Playing with Anxiety: Casey's Guide for Teens and Kids*. You may recall from the introduction that *Casey's Guide* is a free e-book we created specifically for your child, written through the voice of the fictional protagonist in the story, fourteen-year-old Casey. With help from her mom, Casey figured out how to overcome her own problems with anxiety. Now her job is to teach your son or daughter—through her own story as well as analogies and metaphors—how to benefit from the same puzzle pieces you have been studying. Casey models the ways in which a teen or child can develop the courage and independence to win over worry. But she puts no pressure on the reader to face threatening situations. She simply encourages them to consider what a change would be like.

Why are we introducing Casey now? Because our final puzzle piece, coming up in Chapter 12, is all about taking action with your child, and Casey is going to help. Her stories of struggle and success help supplement all that we have explained to you. We have designed her book to intrigue and motivate your child. Chapter 12 in both books walks you through the process of making a plan and stepping into new territory, and Casey's examples prepare you both for this leap.

Directly after Chapter 12 of this book is a segment titled "Using *Casey's Guide* to Help Your Child." There we summarize each chapter of Casey's book and offer a list of discussion questions to help your child learn the principles that Casey presents. After the questions, we offer activities for you and your child—including some playful ones—that reinforce the skills of each puzzle piece.

We also want you and your child to meet Casey because she illustrates an effective yet *playful* approach of responding to anxiety. We chose the title purposefully. To "play with anxiety" has several implications. One is our paradoxical strategy: "Let's fool around with anxiety; let's mess with it." This is a mental game, and you can win over your worries if you have a clever plan that's the opposite of how people typically respond to anxiety. Second, you can play with small aspects of anxiety; you don't have to take any giant steps immediately. Most important, the title implies that the goal shouldn't be to get *rid* of anxiety. You can participate in activities while you are anxious. Most people must tolerate some degree of anxiety and uncertainty as they are learning new skills or facing difficult obstacles.

Based on the age, motivation, and reading level of your child, you have some choices as you begin:

- Do you have a teen or child who is fed up with how anxiety is intruding in her life? Is she, like Casey, eager to turn the tables on worry? If she is independent-minded, a good reader, and already a preteen or teen, she may prefer to read the book on her own (which is a good sign!). Help her get a copy of *Casey's Guide** and let her begin reading. Be sure that you read the book, too. Casey introduces you to some kid-friendly language about worry and anxiety, and she presents stories and illustrations that further solidify your understanding of our principles.

- Younger children may need you to help them read the chapters and explain new words, or you may find it best to read aloud to them. Others might choose to read it on their own. But most young children will be eager for some kind of collaboration with an adult. Together you can set up a schedule to read each chapter and follow through on the questions and activities in "Using *Casey's Guide* to Help Your Child."

Regardless of your child's age, we recommend that you approach your son or daughter with the intent to study and learn together. If you have a willing child, then our suggested approach is as follows:

- Read each chapter, together or independently. We have written *Casey's Guide* to be entertaining enough to keep your child's attention. With that in mind, notice that on most

---

* You may download a free copy of *Casey's Guide* at our website, www.PlayingWithAnxiety.com.

pages, certain phrases are highlighted in bold. In Chapter 1, for instance, here are some examples you will see:

- it helps you run away
- being afraid got him ready
- fear at its finest moment!
- it comes in handy
- slippery, so you can escape
- big, helpful, getting-away muscles
- a dazzle of zebra

If you are reading with a younger child, consider starting each chapter by first scanning through the pages, remarking on the phrases in bold print. We use these to engage your child's curiosity: "I wonder what she means when she says, 'slippery, so you can escape'?"

- Even if you read the chapter separately, schedule time to answer together the questions for that chapter in "Using *Casey's Guide* to Help Your Child." Play the role of a fellow student, not the teacher. Your covert objectives should be to evaluate whether your child is catching on to the principles and to coach her in any arenas where she feels confused or stuck. Let Casey serve as guide, and explore each question as a team by modeling curiosity and the desire to understand the principles behind her stories. ("Let's see if we can figure this one out. . . .")
- Then set aside enough structured time in your week to explore the suggested activities that follow. Entertaining a new perspective is an essential task, but you can't get the job done simply by talking. Experience is the greatest teacher. Your family must step into action. We know that you may be tired

and worn out dealing with worry, so give yourself permission
to have fun as you explore and experiment with these ideas.

- Some teens will have no interest in debriefing each chapter
with you, and they especially don't want to be quizzed by their
parents. You can still act curious about what they are learning,
and you can occasionally ask them to compare notes with you
as you both continue to study.

Putting Down All Fours

When we are afraid, our inclination is to resist. We can act as stubborn as a mule. You know the scene: As the farmer attempts to pull
the mule back into the barn, it puts down all four legs into the dirt
and locks its knees. The farmer can tug with all his might, but that
mule is not budging.

Don't be surprised if your child starts putting down all fours, and
is unwilling to read *Casey's Guide*. Maybe she doesn't even want to
talk about her problem or change anything about how she currently
handles her anxiety and worry.

Now is not the time to coerce her. Instead, start focusing again on
your own work. Return to Chapter 1 and begin (or continue) practicing the activities in the Time to Take Action section. All the concepts
that you study and apply in these first ten chapters are preparing you
to help your child directly face her specific fearful situations.

- Look at your own beliefs and how closely they reflect your
desire to help develop a courageous and independent young
person.
- Think about any of the ways you might be avoiding
uncomfortable situations and how you may unknowingly be

role modeling attitudes and behaviors that are counter
to your child's best interests.
- Use our suggestions to begin planting the seeds of
change in your family.
- Find concrete ways you can role model courage and
independence in the presence of your child.

Once you have confronted your own limitations, shifted the general atmosphere in your family, and encouraged discussions about the themes of this book, you will feel like a stronger parent with clear principles on how to support a courageous and independent teen or child. By then, your child will become accustomed to some new ways of looking at the challenges of the outside world. From this vantage point, you can again approach your child about actively addressing her fearful avoidance.

Your teen or child still won't budge? You don't have to go through this alone. In Appendix B we have listed several national mental health organizations that can help you find someone close to you who specializes in treating childhood anxiety disorders. Appendix A defines those disorders.

Even if you decide to seek professional help from a specialist in childhood anxiety, we encourage you to act on our suggestions within each chapter's Time to Take Action section. All anxiety specialists will want the child's parents to talk and to act in support of the therapeutic strategies. We can assure you that your child's treatment time has a better chance of being shortened, and therefore your financial cost reduced, if you first work through our recommendations in the Time to Take Action sections.

You Might Be Surprised

Casey is going to teach the principles of how to handle worry and face fear. Your child may belong to a special class of young people: those who comprehend the principles well enough that they can immediately and independently apply them to their current problem situations. Casey gives them all the puzzle pieces, and children put them together through courageous effort.

If your child learns to play with anxiety through Casey's help, then you won't need to follow any of our guidelines in Chapter 12. Instead, you can celebrate your child's courage and growing independence. We'll describe this "fast track" at the start of Chapter 12. For kids who need more coaching, the rest of that chapter details a plan for handling specific fears.

12

Moving Toward Courage and Independence

We promised to offer you ways to raise a child who becomes independent. But what are the traits of independent young people? We think of several characteristics as hallmarks. They feel assured in their problem-solving abilities. Even when they are frustrated by a mistake or an inadequacy, they sense that they can learn from addressing the problem. They find at least one or two areas where they experience mastery, giving them a sense of strength, value, and self-confidence. Too, they act because they are motivated to achieve from within, not because of the expectations or demands of others.

Every stage of child development comes with greater independence in the basic areas of living and less reliance on you as a parent. This essential process of separation prepares young people for the demands of adulthood. But they don't gain independence on their own, because they need to be supported by the outlook, abilities, and knowledge of a parent, guardian, or mentor. You don't need to mold a superkid or turn a shy child into an extrovert, or a book lover into an athlete. Your best contributions include giving your children love and respect, guidance to find meaningful and satisfying activities, and then your confidence in their abilities and the gift of freedom to make their own decisions.

For worried children to develop a sense of independence, they must acquire another trait: the willingness to act courageously. Whether their peers have easily mastered the tasks does not matter. When you face any threatening event and you step toward it instead of away from it, you are courageous. Helping your child feel courageous enough to take steps toward their fears—that's the focus of this final chapter.

Is Your Prep Work Done?

In Chapter 11 we primed you for the final puzzle piece that we now introduce: Take Action on Your Plan. You now have in hand all the strategies that dethrone anxiety. If you have applied our suggestions within each chapter's Time to Take Action section, then you've begun to shift how you relate to uncertainties, risk taking, and the normal worries of life. If you and your child have read *Casey's Guide* and worked together on the principles, then it's time to start putting the puzzle pieces together.

As you begin the tasks of this last chapter, keep these points in mind to best prepare you:

- You accept that as your family grows and changes, worry will regularly show up and probably even hang around. But it no longer needs to be the ruler of your family's world.
- You understand worry's predictable attempts to control your family, and you have tools to push back against those interferences.

- You've engaged your child in the process of understanding anxious worries and practiced skills to handle them.
- You've role modeled how to be courageous and how to cope with challenges.
- You've worked to decrease the fearful responses and false alarms that can paralyze parents.
- You certainly know by now that action counts.

So let's now step *toward* worry, help your child create a game plan, and then act on that plan. As you know, your new strategy will be unlike what you and your child have tried in the past. Instead of attempting to create certainty by detailing every aspect of an upcoming experience, answering every question, or addressing all possible outcomes, your aim is to move forward *before* you feel totally comfortable and certain. You needn't go over your plans repeatedly, nor reserve the right to call off the plan if you or your child can't be sure of all outcomes. Instead, support risk taking by applying the principles that each puzzle piece represents.

Anxiety is designed to serve us. But when anxiety dominates instead, it demands that we control the outside circumstances and adjust the environment. "What can the teachers do to make the day smoother? How can we adjust our dinner [travel, work] plans so that our child doesn't worry? Do we have our cell phone available for check-ins?" This is old news by now, isn't it? You have your own examples of how you accommodated anxiety in the past.

Your new plan will focus on your child or teen working toward a different stance: "I can handle what happens. Even though I've never been here before, I can find my way. What past experiences will help me figure this out? I can rely on my problem solving to move forward. I can use calming breaths to reboot my body and mind. I can feel unsure as I step into this scene." You know that we cannot control the outside world, so invest in a game plan that allows your family to respond, learn, and adapt. When anxiety and worry no longer call the shots, your family can focus on handling all sorts of new and challenging situations. By pointing yourselves toward what you want out of life, not away from what you hope to avoid, you start to move through those challenges and uncertainties of life.

A FASTER TRACK

Some of you are reading this and nodding along. You might even be feeling impatient to begin addressing your child's current problems. "We get it! We're ready. Thanks for your help. Now let us go!" If you're dealing with teens, they may want to—and even should—be given the freedom to move ahead independently. Who are we to stand in the way? You have our support.

Some kids and teens take what they learn from Casey and charge ahead, knowing they'll have some worries and fears along the way.

Allow them to step into the unpredictable arenas of their lives. Let them jump or slide or wander into moments of sweaty palms, pounding heart, uncertainty, and mistakes. Over time they will equip themselves with the core strategies to win:

- They know the important tasks that they want to accomplish.
- They remember past successes that can help them face new challenges.
- They expect worry to show up.
- They talk to their worries so that anxiety doesn't run the show.
- They step on into new situations.
- They are willing to feel unsure and uncomfortable along the way.
- They use their breathing skills to support them.

If your son or daughter is ready to apply the principles of *Casey's Guide,* then your job of protecting and reassuring and running interference for your child will slowly disappear. This is good news, of course. What can you put in place of your old job? Be curious and available to talk. Check in and be supportive. They're playing the game, and you're no longer coaching, just cheering from the sidelines. Of course, we encourage *you* to keep reading this chapter for more insights on how to support your child in the future.

SHIFTING INTO ACTION

Children who are more hesitant prefer to take a gradual approach to putting the game plan into action, and they will need your support. A few more warm-ups. A bit of rehearsal. We understand that, and we think it is a much better approach than for a parent to try to coerce a resistant child into confronting threatening situations prematurely. That's why we ask you first to engage your child with the questions and activities of the next section of the book, "Using *Casey's Guide* to Help Your Child." No pushing kids into the deep end before they've had swimming lessons!

Going slow is reasonable, but the research is clear: children and parents must take action in order to retrain the fearful child's brain and to start experiencing different outcomes within the family. To help your child move toward independence and courage, together pick a current situation that causes distress. Then we suggest you take these active steps:

1. Review the puzzle pieces.
2. Create an imaginary worry scenario and talk through each puzzle piece.
3. Repeat the process with a past situation.
4. Create a plan and take action on the distressing event.

Review the Puzzle Pieces

Write down each of the seven puzzle pieces on a separate index card: EXPECT TO WORRY, TALK TO WORRY, BE UNSURE AND UNCOMFORTABLE ON PURPOSE, BREATHE!, KNOW WHAT YOU WANT, BRIDGE BACK TO YOUR SUCCESSES, and TAKE ACTION ON YOUR PLAN. Talk to your child about the puzzle pieces, helping each other to remember examples or stories that illustrate the concept. ("I expected to be nervous when I met my new boss," or "I told my worry to leave me alone when I was taking my German exam.") If each of you has read *Casey's Guide*, recall the stories that Casey told to explain each puzzle piece. Has your child already had success using any of the puzzle pieces? What about others in the family?

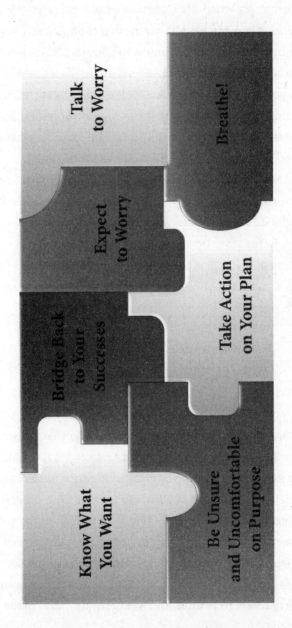

The Big Picture of Beating Anxiety

On each card, write a few phrases or sentences as reminders of how the puzzle piece works. For example, on EXPECT TO WORRY you might write, "Worry is going to show up. It's a normal part of growing." Or for BRIDGE BACK TO YOUR SUCCESSES you could write something like, "Worry makes me forget by sprinkling worry dust on my brain. But when I focus on my successes, worry gets smaller." Allow your child to illustrate the cards in whatever way she chooses.

Keep these cards around for review and as reminders. Some families put them in places where they might be immediately helpful—under pillows, in backpacks, with the nurse or guidance counselor at school, in the glove box of the car. Teens may prefer to write a list of the steps on a single piece of paper or card. Let them decide what works best for them. Also, consider posting a list of the puzzle pieces on the refrigerator.

Create an Imaginary Worry Scenario and Talk Through Each Puzzle Piece

With your child, choose an anxiety-provoking scene to practice putting the puzzle pieces together. Find one that is not directly related to her specific worries (that comes soon enough, in step 4). Invent a fictional character who is working through a challenge, or call upon a situation that you've heard about from others, or even something that your child's peer has dealt with (nothing too threatening, please). Using the cards as reminders, describe how each puzzle piece can be applied to meet that challenge. How might the character shift from avoiding to stepping into uncertainty? How does worry try to get control, and what can the "hero" of the story do to succeed in the face of worry?

Because we all learn better through engaging experiences, help make this story absorbing enough to keep your child involved as you create the plan. Be playful or a bit silly, or use characters with whom your child can relate. Some might enjoy making a storybook, a video, or even a PowerPoint presentation of the tale. Using such an imagined scenario removes any performance pressure and allows children to move through the process without their own anxious themes getting in the way. Teens may be more inclined to talk it through, and that's okay, too. The goal is to invest enough time and effort into the process for your son or daughter to perceive the potential benefits of putting the puzzle pieces together. This does not need to be done all at once. You can take your time to make it meaningful.

Back in Chapter 5 we talked about the content trap. The key to remember here is that worried kids tend to pull you into the specific content of their worries, and that will slow down or even derail this early stage of learning. Right now, your job is to help your child step away from the specific fear in order to grasp how one can handle worry in *any* situation. Practicing without the heft of threatening content enables them to experiment and learn. You'll hit a bit more resistance in step 4, when you address one of their personal issues. The more work you do now to help them comprehend the generic skills, the less opposition you will face later.

An eleven-year-old boy with social anxiety created the following story and plan. He had just started taking guitar lessons, so his topic selection is not surprising. It's close enough, but still far enough away from his circumstances to be a safe choice. We added the italics to highlight his use of each puzzle piece in his story.

***

Jack Diamond was a very good guitar player. He started playing guitar when he was eleven, and he always wanted to be in a rock band and play concerts all over the world. Finally, his dream came true, and he was going to play with his band in front of a huge crowd at a concert in New York City. It was the biggest concert of his life. He was very nervous. He even thought about quitting the band!

When Jack Diamond was a kid, he had anxiety. He didn't talk to the teachers at school, and he never went to sleepovers. But his guitar teacher taught him a plan to use so that he could play his guitar in front of people. He knew this was the time to use his plan, so he remembered the seven puzzle pieces.

First, he *expected to worry*. Of course worry would show up. It was the biggest concert of his life! When he was rehearsing for the concert, worry started telling him that he was going to screw up and maybe even forget how to play the guitar. Jack Diamond was not going to let his worry *boss him around*. "I'm sick of you trying to tell me what to do! I kicked you out when I was eleven, and I'll do it again right now!" Then Jack took some *calming breaths*. His alarm system had already been called into action a bit. He wanted to remind himself and his brain that he could be nervous, but this was not an emergency. He didn't need his amygdala getting all crazy. Then he remembered what his old guitar teacher told him. If he wanted to be a rock star, he had to *be willing to be uncomfortable* and even scared at times. Good! He was scared to play in front of all these people, but that's what rock stars do! He practiced his *calming breaths* again so that he could use them on stage. That was easy! Then he reminded himself *what he wanted*. That was even easier! He wanted to be a rock star. If worry stayed in charge, he would never be able to do this. His teacher also told him that worry makes you forget your successes, so at night, when he was falling asleep, he would *remember* all the times he learned new songs or played in front of people. He remembered when he had his first job playing at a small hotel. He was nervous, but he did it, and now that seemed like no big deal. Jack Diamond knew he had a *good plan.* He remembered all the pieces, practiced his breathing, and let himself imagine how awesome he would feel on stage with people cheering.

But he did one more thing: he wrote down all the puzzle pieces on his arm before he went onto the big stage in New York City. Everyone probably thought he was writing down the names of the songs, but he knew better. Whenever he felt nervous, he looked at his arm, and that reminded him what to do. He played the concert, and it was awesome. He made tons of money and lived in a mansion and had a Mustang. It's a good thing his worry didn't get in the way.

Repeat the Process with a Past Situation

Your child now has a chance for a redo. Help her identify a situation that she struggled with previously but is not currently a problem. Discuss how she might respond differently to that past event if she actively engaged in each of the seven puzzle pieces. If your child has difficulty addressing a past problem, consider sharing a prior difficulty of your own, and then draw her into a conversation comparing and contrasting your problems. If you could relive that event while applying the principles of the seven puzzle pieces, how might your experience change? How might the choices each of you make be similar or different (but remember that your child is not *your* helper or problem solver). As you both look back, can you see where and when worry showed up? How did it stay in control? What did it say? When you recognize worry's tactics and then change your responses, how does that influence the outcome?

Create a Plan and Take Action on the Distressing Event

Once your child has prepared the cards, or a reminder list for older teens, and practiced with both a fictional and a past scenario, select together a real-life issue that is challenging for your child. The process remains the same: to imagine a scenario of your child engaging in that event sometime in the future and then, guided by the puzzle pieces, to envisage how the scene could unfold. Keep the focus on what your child can do to keep moving forward.

Using the chart that follows, help your child identify multiple goals she has—activities that are important or fun or interesting—that are limited by worry and avoidance. Then list the steps she thinks she will need to take in order to arrive at each goal. (You can review Frannie's steps for starting horseback riding lessons in Chapter 9 to remind you of the process.)

Next, help your child pick out an initial goal to work toward. Minimally, focus on finding an inspiring want-to, like we discussed in Chapter 9. As your child prepares to take action—which requires responding to worries and moving forward even when she feels like stepping back—she'll need a motivating reward in the forefront of her thinking. Here's the formula we described to help your child embrace the steps of a difficult but desired goal: "Since I want [desired outcome], then I'm willing to [take this less-than-desirable step] to get there."

If several choices include strong want-tos, then how do you select the best issue to tackle first? This decision is more of a personal one. Perhaps she'll opt for the one that feels easiest, so she can build trust in the process and confidence in her abilities, or she might pick the goal that she is most motivated to reach, because of social or academic significance. Maybe she'll choose one that occurs frequently and feels most intrusive, or one that she knows you'll understand the most. Some parents want their child to start with the smallest issue and work up to a more daunting one, but if your child is motivated to go after a bigger worry and has done the preparation, go for it!

Steps Toward an Important Goal

What is something that you want? An important goal to reach?	List the steps it will take to get there. Be specific.

As you look for this first goal, be aware that children tend to employ stalling tactics in this planning phase, as their anxiety creeps in and demands that they are "completely ready" before moving into the actual scenario. Remind your child that *being unsure and uncomfortable on purpose* is the puzzle piece that helps keep both of you moving. If your child puts worry in charge, he's going to want to stay safe, which means you're both going to stay stuck. The message to convey here is that although worry wants us to wait and wait until we're comfortable with the plan, we're going to move forward anyway, bringing our uncertainty with us. No puzzle piece says, "Wait! We're still uncomfortable!"

Once your child chooses a goal, she is ready to move through each puzzle piece and then complete the Game Plan worksheet. Back in Chapter 6, we introduced you to ten-year-old Christie, who worried about falling asleep without a parent staying in her bedroom. She provides us with a good example of how to take advantage of each puzzle piece and use the worksheet to create her plan. We began by asking her, "What do you want, and how will worry try to get in your way? What will you do each step of the way?" Putting the puzzle together, she wrote,

✳ ✳ ✳

Know What You Want. I want to have our nights go smoother. I want us to stop yelling at each other at night. My parents aren't getting good sleep, and I'm not either. I want to be able to wake up and get going in the morning, and not feel so sleepy and grumpy from a bad night's sleep. I want to be able to read my chapter book for a bit and then go to sleep like my friends do.

Bridge Back to Your Successes. I can think back to all the skills I have, and how I learned them by practicing. I can remember when I didn't know how to read, and how I had to start with easy books. Now I can read chapter books by myself. I used to make Mom ride in the backseat with me in the car when Dad was driving, and now that seems silly to me. I learned to handle that.

Expect to Worry. Worry will show up when I start getting ready for bed, or it might show up during dinner. It will tell me I can't do it or get me to think about scary stuff. It will do what it always does. Nothing new. I will expect it because we are making a change.

Talk to Worry. I'll tell worry that I'm *not* going to follow its orders anymore. I'll tell worry that even though I'm scared, I am going to handle being in my room and not believe what it says.

Take Action on Your Plan. I'm stepping into this with a plan! I have an index card under my pillow with what I can say back to worry. I am going to get a really great chapter book at the bookstore and read that before I fall asleep. I might even write the seven puzzle pieces inside the front cover. When worry shows up, I will just remember how great it is to read independently at night. If I start imagining scary pictures, I will remind myself that worry wants me to call Mom, but I can shift my thoughts and my breathing. If I can't fall asleep right away, I can even try reading a bit more. Mom said that's okay as I learn to do this. If I call Mom, she's going to remind me to use my puzzle pieces, but she's not going to come into my room.

Be Unsure and Uncomfortable on Purpose. I am probably going to feel nervous and scared because that's what I've been doing for a long time. But if I can get through that feeling, and talk to my worry, then I will be able to show my brain that I can handle this. It's okay to get nervous. That's how my brain learns and that's how I practice. When worry tells me to look under the bed and check the closet over and over again, I will tell it that I'm not playing that game anymore. I want to make bedtime easier, so I'm willing to feel scared for a while as I use my plan. (And for you, parents: I want us all to get better sleep, so I'm willing to be uncomfortable and to let Mom be uncomfortable and struggle a bit as she learns this.)

Breathe! I know how to calm my body with my breath. That reminds me to use my prefrontal cortex and stops my amygdala from firing off. When I do my calming breaths, I reboot my system and give myself a chance to think and problem solve. The breathing skills help me take a break and remember my plan.

✳✳✳

Christie then filled out the Game Plan worksheet, which helped further clarify her goal and spell out the actions needed to tackle her problem. She practiced her plan by spending some time in her bedroom over several afternoons. She rested on the bed and used her breathing skills while she read her new chapter book. Occasionally she would stop reading, take her reminders out from under her pillow, and review them. She imagined what worry might say at night. And she prepared by talking out loud to her worry so that she could hear herself say the words.

Below is a copy of Christie's completed Game Plan worksheet and a blank one for you and your child to use. Your child may benefit from watching you fill out the worksheet for one of your (child-friendly) struggles and then use the worksheet for one of her own issues. If possible, help your child come up with some ways to practice parts of the plan ahead of time, just as Christie did. We encourage you to make several copies of this blank Game Plan and use it often as a guide for taking on difficult tasks. Over time, the worksheet will become unnecessary as the family internalizes the process. With repetition, you will all master the ability to reach inside for the tools needed to handle anxiety when it arrives.

The Game Plan

What is your goal?

Go to bed on my own and fall asleep without Mom in the bed or the room.

Do you really want this goal?

☐ No, it's not important to me.

☑ Yes. I want it, but I'm not sure I can get there.

What skills do you need to reach your goal?

(1) Be willing to be alone. (2) Stay in bed and use my cards and my book. (3) Talk to myself when I'm worried. (4) Take some calming breaths when I need them.

What do you already know how to do that might help you reach this goal?

I know how to use my imagination when I read, and I really do know how to fall asleep because I do it every night!

What do you want to say to yourself when you start to worry?

'Worry tells me I can't do it, but I can. I can read my book and wait until I feel tired. I will feel a little uncomfortable, but I can get through it with some practice.'

Are you willing not to know exactly how things will turn out?

☐ NO! I HAVE to know or I don't want to do it!

☑ Yes. I might not like it, but I'll use my courage.

Are you willing to feel physically uncomfortable along the way?

☐ NO! I HAVE to be calm or I won't do it!

☑ Yes. I might not like it, but I'll use my courage.

What can you do to practice your skills?

Look over my cards, read in my bed in the afternoon and practice talking to worry, make sure I have a great book to read! Practice my calming breaths to slow me down when I want to remember my plan.

The Game Plan

What is your goal?

_____

_____

Do you really want this goal?

☐ No, it's not important to me.

☐ Yes. I want it, but I'm not sure I can get there.

What skills do you need to reach your goal?

_____

_____

What do you already know how to do that might help you reach this goal?

_____

_____

What do you want to say to yourself when you start to worry?

_____

_____

Are you willing not to know exactly how things will turn out?

☐ NO! I HAVE to know or I don't want to do it!

☐ Yes. I might not like it, but I'll use my courage.

Are you willing to feel physically uncomfortable along the way?

☐ NO! I HAVE to be calm or I won't do it!

☐ Yes. I might not like it, but I'll use my courage.

What can you do to practice your skills?

_____

_____

Answering the worksheet questions and writing down goals helps your child think concretely about what he wants and how to get there. The yes and no questions "force" him to accept or reject the principles (and hard work) required to change: Does he have a goal that's important enough? Is he willing to feel uncertain and uncomfortable along the way? When he can answer yes to each of these, you'll know that he understands the principles and is willing to take some risk.

But what if he answers no to one of the questions? This answer could indicate that your child doesn't yet feel equipped enough to step into uncertainty and needs more practice putting the puzzle pieces together. It may also mean that he hasn't identified a goal important enough to justify the work to come. He may perceive the goal as too big or overwhelming and thus views it as impossible. Now's the time to again think about *process over content*. If he has several want-to goals on his chart, look for a goal that seems to have less difficult steps. If he can back up a bit to a less threatening set of tasks (the *content*) in order to get the three yeses checked, he will then have the opportunity to practice the general *process* of handling fear and worry and to have a successful experience along the way. So if his ultimate goal is to go to sleep-away summer camp for two weeks, but he hasn't yet been able to sleep at his grandmother's house for one night, then practice that goal first, using the puzzle pieces to help him reach this intermediate step.

But remember this: *No one moves ahead by waiting to feel totally certain and comfortable.* If your child consistently answers no to the second or third questions—"Are you willing not to know exactly how things will turn out?" and "Are you willing to feel physically uncomfortable along the way?"—then go back to Chapters 6 and 7 in both this book and *Casey's Guide* to review the stories, principles, and exercises of the puzzle piece BE UNSURE AND UNCOMFORTABLE ON PURPOSE. These worksheet questions serve an important function: to make sure you and your child understand this vital component of the plan. We perceive it as a cornerstone of our treatment with both young people and adults, and we emphasize it with everyone we see.

As therapists, we usually say this to a not-so-enthusiastic child: "We seem to get stuck on those yes-or-no questions. What do you think we can do together to turn those nos into yeses?" We problem solve together and sometimes elect to introduce an incentive or two. Keep reading.

PAYING FOR PROGRESS

Of course, when you read success stories, it all sounds so easy, doesn't it? Your child buys into our approach and cooperates, and your lives improve immediately. Can that happen? Absolutely. We've seen it over and over again. But it's probably more realistic to expect obstacles to cross and refusals to manage as you and your child change some entrenched patterns. Using these tools takes practice, and setbacks happen. But we know from our own work and from the clinical research that *frequent, consistent engagement* with the anxiety-provoking situation is the best approach. So let's talk about how to handle those bumps and keep the momentum going. Let's talk bribery.

Rewards are a part of life. We give our kids an allowance, and the neighbor pays them to mow the lawn or babysit. We get a paycheck and buy a car with the promise of "cash back"! Ideally, we'd love our children to understand that living independently is reward enough, without material prizes as an incentive. But the reality is this: we engage in specific activities because of the rewards we get. Wanting a reward for a job well done is perfectly normal, so part of the plan can include some kind of prize. In Chapter 9 we talked about identifying a meaningful want-to, but sometimes a want-to such as, "I want to go to school with my friends" or "I want to succeed when I go off to college" can feel too big or far away. Adding some short-term incentives along the way can help keep kids moving and give them something concrete to strive for while they work toward the bigger prize. "I want an extra thirty minutes of television time" or "I want Chinese food on Friday night" can be rewards for steps taken in the right direction.

When you and your child make a plan, include some fun incentives. One goal of a young boy working on his social anxiety was to respond to adult greetings at school with eye contact and a firm "Hello!" The adults in his life had a grander want-to in mind—be able to interact with adults and peers in school—but his plan focused on getting a pizza after ten successful greetings. Christie's sleeping-on-my-own plan included a trip to the new bookstore after completing several nights without Mom in the room.

Follow these guidelines for including rewards with the plan:

- Keep the rewards smaller and more frequent. Requiring several weeks to earn a reward won't sustain motivation for most anxious kids.

- Set up rewards for practicing. Start with *any* of the tasks we have suggested in this chapter. If you sit together with your child to review the puzzle pieces before bed, he earns a point! If he practices talking back to worry as he's getting ready for school, he earns a point!

- The younger the child, the more frequent the reward. For kids under the age of ten, awarding little prizes daily seems to work best. Teens can handle (and want) longer wait times in order to earn bigger payoffs.

- We prefer "activity" rewards to "stuff" rewards, but we'll leave that decision up to you.

- *Never* take away a reward (or a point or a star or a sticker) once it's been earned.

- *Never* include a punishment or penalty if a goal is not achieved.

- Do not create a reward system that demands "days in a row." This is too much pressure and will demoralize your child quickly. Instead of "ten days sleeping on your room in a row and then we go out to dinner," go with "when you have five nights sleeping in your room, we'll go out to dinner," even if it takes twenty nights to get there!

- Be specific. Rather than rewarding five "good days" (too general), go with "five days when you don't go to the nurse's office and ask to call Mom." Or five days with no texts during school.

- Create a rewards chart. Then keep it visible, so everyone remembers.

- Two to three weeks is about as long as kids and parents stay interested in a specific set of rewards within a behavioral plan, so be prepared to change it up frequently. Adjust the goal a bit; change the reward . . . *anything* to rekindle interest. You don't need to change the whole plan after two to three weeks, just the specific goal or reward, or both.

THE CHALLENGES OF A FULL LIFE

You have now put all seven puzzle pieces together, and you have the know-how to make big changes in your family. Our goal has been to give you and your children the keys to a new stance on anxiety, and we hope that after thinking about and practicing these skills, you realize that we are *not* teaching you how to *get rid of* anxiety. When people ask us if anxiety is curable, we emphatically say yes, because "curable" to us means the ability to accept and manage this basic human experience. Anxiety is a natural and often helpful part of living, so consider your efforts here as practice for handling your family's inevitably unpredictable future.

We build independence and the strength of courage by learning to tolerate uncertainty, to problem solve effectively, to step into uncomfortable situations, and to manage both risk and failure. Every child or teen—anxious or not—will benefit from these skills. We all continue to face difficulties as we move through the life cycle. We hope that you and your children both now have a process that, once mastered, enables your family to handle the challenges that a full life offers.

TIME TO TAKE ACTION:
Applying the Concepts of Chapter Twelve

Just for Parents

1. Now that you have come to the end of these chapters, spend some time thinking about how your understanding of and approach to anxiety have changed. What are you already doing differently with your children? What do you now know about the worry cycle that is in complete contrast to what you once believed? What new information do you predict will most impact your parenting? Your own functioning?

2. We have just suggested using rewards to help keep your child motivated and engaged. Have you used rewards and punishments in your family in the past? What worked well? What didn't? Often a parent's first response to refusal and passivity is to punish, but taking away cell phones or privileges does not teach a skill. You've felt frustrated in the past, and we know you'll get frustrated in the future, but staying calm and focusing on positive gains support your child's momentum forward instead of building her resentment. If you have struggled to be consistent with a reward plan, then we offer some additional tips to help stay on track:

   - Keep it simple and visual. We like using bright-colored stickies on a visible wall of the house to keep track of goals met.
   - Avoid multi-tiered plans like, "If you get five stickies, you can stay up ten minutes later, and then when you get to ten stickies we'll order a pizza." That's too complicated. Make

one goal with one reward. After your child gets five stickies (or whatever you decide), take them down and start over, or move them to another section of the victory wall so that everyone can see the progress.

- That said, change up that one reward frequently, and change the goal when mastery has been achieved. Is brushing teeth alone in the bathroom no longer an issue? Then adjust the goal accordingly. But again, the "one goal, one reward" guideline makes life easier.

- If your goal or rewards are not working, not interesting, or just not helping, talk as a family about what you can change to get back on track. It's fine to adjust the strategy as needed. Don't let an ineffective or worn-out reward lead to abandoning the whole plan. All-or-nothing thinking will stop you in your tracks.

- If you believe that creating a reward system and following through consistently is too much work, think for a moment about how much time and energy the anxiety in your family demands of you.

- Do not punish. Do not threaten. Do not take away a reward that has been earned. It doesn't work.

USING *CASEY'S GUIDE* TO HELP YOUR CHILD

CHAPTER 1:
A GLOB OF CATERPILLARS

In this first chapter, Casey explains the difference between being *familiar* with worry and *understanding* worry, and how she and her mom decided to approach her worry as a puzzle they need to solve. Anxious kids certainly know what it feels like to worry. But here your child learns how worry serves an important purpose. That understanding makes the whole process less mysterious. Casey explains how worry and fear protect us from danger, and uses both the instincts and clever maneuvers of animals to illustrate the fight-or-flight response (like zebras, that have stripes so that when they zigzag through the savannah, they create an optical illusion that confuses predators).

Problems mentioned in this chapter include being afraid of going to school, falling off your bike, vomiting before a recital, and feeling frightened of aggressive dogs.

Reviewing Chapter 1 with Your Child

Questions to Discuss with Your Child

1. What happened to Casey that made her determined to learn about worry and how to handle it?

2. What's the difference between being familiar with something and understanding it? What did Casey give as examples?

3. Can you think of something that you're familiar with, but don't really understand? *(Grown-ups can give examples, too.)*

4. What are some ways that Casey's mom helped Casey avoid? Which ones seemed to make worry bigger?

5. How did Boo's body respond when he ran into the dog? How did Casey's body respond when she was scared and sensed danger? Why do bodies do that? Why do they do it so *quickly*? Do we get to pick and choose when our bodies react to a scary situation?

6. In what ways can worry *help* us? Can you think of a situation in which listening to worry is a smart idea?

7. What are some of the interesting ways that animals protect themselves? What does a zebra do? A skunk? A beaver? What do your pets do?

Chapter 1 Activities with Your Child

1. Talk with your child about what made you both decide to take charge of worry at this time. Why not three months ago? Why not wait until next year? Your reasons may not be the same, and each of you may cite different past or future events that motivate you. Of course, your child may not have decided to change yet. If she is unsure, can you discuss how this *might* be a good time?

2. Search out information about a few more animals that cleverly protect themselves. (Check out the "mimic octopus"!)

3. Divide a piece of paper in half by drawing a line down the middle, from top to bottom. On one side, write down four or five situations where worry was helpful. On the other side, list other situations where worry was a problem and got in the way. Like this:

Situations Where Worry Was Helpful	Situations Where Worry Was a Problem
I remembered to put on my helmet before I got on my bike.	*I missed Jane's birthday party because I was afraid her older brother might dress up like a clown. All my friends went, and then they talked in school about how fun the party was. And her brother didn't even dress up!*

After completing that list, discuss how we don't have to get *rid* of worry (it shows up automatically when it thinks we need help; everybody has worries), and it's okay to ignore worried thoughts when they aren't useful. We only need to pay attention to worry when it's helpful in that specific situation.

CHAPTER 2:
DON'T CLIMB THAT TREE!

Casey talks about how the combination of genetics and parenting may influence whether kids become anxious and worried. Genes can affect how much a child struggles with worry, but parenting style has a big impact as well. Parents might be worriers themselves, and they often want to keep their kids comfortable and safe. She introduces a key paradoxical concept: when parents and kids work hard to stay *comfortable* and to *avoid* worry or uncertainty, then worry gets bigger.

Stories that illustrate this chapter include how physical traits in the O'Donnell family are different from those in Casey's family, the shy qualities of her friend Lizzie, and how her mom can sometimes act in an overprotective manner.

Reviewing Chapter 2 with Your Child

Questions to Discuss with Your Child

1. What are genes? Name some traits that seem to be passed down in your family through genes (examples: eye color, height, baldness).

2. Name some tendencies or characteristics that were passed down in your family, but might have been *taught* and not inherited. (A recipe? A holiday tradition? A favorite team?)

3. What did Casey's mom learn about anxiety and parents? Why was that hard for her to hear?

4. Casey tells us some ways that her mom made worry stronger for her and for Elliot. What were some things she did? (If they can't remember, turn back through the pages together and look for the illustration.)

5. How does avoiding make *you* feel better? And how does it make *worry* stronger?

6. What are some of the activities that Casey avoided?

7. Is there anything you *don't* like about avoiding? Any activity you miss out on that you'd eventually like to do?

Chapter 2 Activities with Your Child

1. Make a list with your child and other family members of any ways worry might control the family. What routines or rituals support avoidance in your family? (Having Mom drive the kids to school to avoid the school bus, going to the movies late to avoid the loud previews, always going to the same restaurant to avoid unfamiliar menus, making grandparents babysit to avoid babysitters.)

2. Have you heard of swearing jars, where a quarter must be deposited whenever someone uses a bad word? Create a "safety chatter" jar. Tell your children that they get to fine you a quarter every time your worry jumps in to parent them. *The nonanxious adults in the house get to fine you, too. They can be very helpful once given permission to point out the anxious role modeling.* List the kind of messages that deserve a fine. ("Be careful with that knife! You could cut your finger off!" "Remember there are bees outside, and you could get stung!" "I'm not going to leave you home alone, because someone could steal you!")

CHAPTER 3:
STOP THE WORLD, I WANT TO GET OFF

Casey continues to explain why kids worry. Three ingredients—stress, an amazing imagination, and being too rigid—can each make worry stronger by sending a signal to stop. The busyness of life has a way of overwhelming kids. Thinking about and imagining the possibility of bad events happening can also generate worries. When children believe that they should be perfect or that there is only one right way to do an activity, then they become as rigid as an uncooked spaghetti noodle. That's the opposite of the flexibility (a cooked noodle) that helps kids cope. Casey offers several common examples of how children learn by trial and error. She helps children see the power of their imaginations and how they might harness that power in more positive ways. In fact, she explains how most of what we learn as children involves trying and failing and trying again.

Problems in this chapter include being overwhelmed by stimuli, fear of spending the night away from home, and Casey's perfectionistic tendencies during her fourth-grade owl project.

Reviewing Chapter 3 with Your Child

Questions to Discuss with Your Child

1. What did Casey look like after her stressful afternoon at her friend's house?

2. What situations make Casey and her mom (and lots of other people) feel stressed out?

3. How can an active imagination make anxiety stronger?

4. How did Elliot's comic book help Casey learn about her imagination and her worry?

5. Why does Casey think worried kids are like uncooked spaghetti?

6. How did Casey's need to be "perfect" get in the way of her learning?

7. Why are mistakes important for kids?

Chapter 3 Activities with Your Child

The activities here will help you and your child identify areas where anxious rigidity might be in charge and guide you as you practice more flexibility in the family.

1. Each day for a week, change an activity that is routine (or even rigid) in your house. (Change the seating arrangements at the dinner table. Make the beds with the pillow at the opposite end. Serve ice cream for dinner.)

2. Make a list of times when being rigid with a rule is necessary (wearing a helmet when riding a bike, fastening your seat belt in the car) and times when flexibility about rules is okay (a later bedtime when cousins are visiting, skipping homework when you're battling a tough cold).

3. Ask three or four adults to describe their "perfect" vacation and "perfect" dessert.

4. Talk with your child about ways that your imaginations have affected your bodies. When does your heart beat a little faster? When might you blush? What makes your stomach feel funny? What can you think about that makes you feel energetic? Tired? Hungry?

5. Using the examples below, talk about when you might want to push harder to get better and when being "less than perfect" is good enough, perhaps even preferred.

    a. Handwriting
    b. Measuring
    c. Walking
    d. Singing
    e. Trying something difficult for the very first time

6. Create a Wall of Flexibility. Choose a section of visible wall somewhere in the house (a door works well, too). Get a bunch of fun sticky notes. Every time someone in the family demonstrates flexibility (managing a change in routine, compromising with a sibling, trying a new activity), write down a few descriptive words on

the sticky and put it up on the wall for all to see. Agree as a family how many stickies must be on the wall to earn a fun activity. With smaller children, we like to start with ten; older kids can go for twenty.

CHAPTER 4:
GREAT EXPECTATIONS

Casey reviews the reasons that kids worry:

- Worry helps them *slow down* when it's smart to take their time, *back away* from activities when it's smart to avoid, and *run away or fight* when the danger is real.
- Some kids are more likely to worry because of their biological makeup.
- Parents may unknowingly teach worrying by the ways they act.
- The world can be a fast and stressful place, and sometimes kids take on too much.
- Kids can imagine all kinds of scary problems.
- Some kids think that they need all events to work out perfectly. When they're not sure how an activity will turn out, their need for everything to turn out "just right" causes them to worry.

Casey then moves into the plan for handling anxiety with the first piece of the puzzle: EXPECT TO WORRY. Kids should assume they will worry in certain situations, like when doing a new activity or when performing in front of people. They then gain a better sense of control by *expecting* worry to show up rather than being surprised by it. Worry always believes it is being helpful and protective, even when it's not. Kids can learn the right times to stop and pay attention to their worries. They can also learn when to ignore those normal, expected worried thoughts and move on with life.

Reviewing Chapter 4 with Your Child

Questions to Discuss with Your Child

1. What are the five reasons that kids might worry?

2. What did Casey worry about at the water park? Did her worries ruin her fun?

3. What is the first puzzle piece that Casey teaches?

4. Casey came up with five times when any of us tend to worry.
   • What are they?
   • Name two topics that Casey worried about and two topics that Elliot worried about.
   • For each of the five times that we tend to worry, name something that makes you worry, too.

5. Casey tells us that worry *will* show up, but we don't have to let it "run the show." When kids let worry run the show, what might they do differently? What might they miss out on?

Chapter 4 Activities with Your Child

1. Talk about examples when someone *should* listen to a worry message, as well as other times when a worry message might show up but can be ignored. Talk generally about lots of different scenarios, and don't limit your examples to typical real-life situations. Use your creative imaginations, and let your silliness come out. ("When you are going down a hill on your bike and your worry tells you to use your brakes and slow down, you should listen to

that worry." But . . . "When you go to bed and worry tells you that squirrels are going to steal your swing set during the night, you should ignore that worry.")

2. Come up with examples when kids are surprised by an event that they should expect. ("Joey was surprised when our teacher gave us homework, even though we're in fifth grade now!" Or "Tyler was surprised when Aunt Lucille gave him pajamas for his birthday, even though she *always* gives us pajamas for our birthdays!")

3. Together, ask other adults and family members about situations where worried thoughts show up for them. Create a blank worksheet like this one to help categorize the worries, like Casey and Elliot did.

Where Do Worried Thoughts Show Up?

Trying a New Activity	Unsure of Your Plans	You Have a Lot of "What If" Questions	You Have to Perform for People	Something Scary Is Happening

CHAPTER 5:
CHATTING WITH THE SQUIRREL

Worry is a normal part of life. When it shows up, you need a variety of flexible responses, not one rigid reaction. After identifying and expecting worry, Casey now teaches kids how to externalize and TALK TO THEIR WORRY, the next piece of the puzzle.

Casey used to believe that all her thoughts and fears were important . . . until she met another girl who had far less patience for bothersome worry and showed Casey how to talk back to it when it gets too bossy. You can choose how you talk to worry; sometimes you can act annoyed and other times sympathetic. Casey illustrates how she put this strategy to work when she was studying for her recent math test, how Elliot used it to get back in the swing of baseball, and how friend Kate applied it to handling her bedtime anxieties.

Reviewing Chapter 5 with Your Child

Questions to Discuss with Your Child

1. What is the second puzzle piece?

2. What animal did the girl in the doctor's office use for her worry? What animal did Casey use for hers?

3. How does Casey's friend Kate handle her bedtime worry?

4. How does worry bother Elliot? What does he do to externalize his worry and talk back to it?

5. What are the different ways that kids can talk to worry?

6. Casey tells us that we can't "banish" worry. What does Casey mean by that?

7. If we can't get *rid* of worry, what do we need to do instead?

Chapter 5 Activities with Your Child

1. You can help your child create a name for her worry. After reading Casey's chapter, she may have some ideas of her own or might choose to borrow Casey's squirrel or the mouse from the girl in the doctor's office. Some kids like to have a tangible object. Drawing a picture, using clay, buying a toy figure, or simply giving it a name is great. If your child gets stuck, come up with a name for your own worry. You can even ask your child if she'd like to borrow yours for a bit until she comes up with her own.

Some Names for Worry

Worry Channel	Mr. Panic	Fear Gremlin
Exaggerator	Brain Bug	Nervous Neddy
Worry Glitch	Worry Bug	Mr. Negative
Panic Ogre	Troll	Alarm Button
Ms. Dread	Mr. Right	Worry Tape
OCD	Germy	Worry Bully
Interrupter	Worry Brain	Mrs. Watch-It
Dr. No		

2. Practice the different ways of talking to worry. Use several generic examples of worries that are not issues for your child, so that the content of the example doesn't trigger anxiety or avoidance. In other words, use something *easy* so he'll learn the skill and stay engaged with Casey's ideas and the puzzle pieces. If you have a family dog, for example, and your child has no fear of dogs, then that would be good practice content. Use the table below as a guide and fill in the empty boxes. We use dogs and going to camp as "practice content" examples.

Talking Back to Worry

Specific Worry	Expect Worry	Take Care of Worry	Boss Worry Around
Scared of dogs	There's a dog, so of course worry will start talking to me about it. Worry is so predictable.	Worry, I know dogs can scare me, but I know what to do around dogs.	Worry, I'm tired of you stopping me from doing things just because a dog might be there. I'm not listening!
Afraid of overnight camp	Oh, hi, worry. I knew you'd show up because I'm heading off to camp.	Worry, we'll have fun at camp. It just takes me a day to settle in, like last year.	Worry, I love camp, and I'm not going to let you get in my way anymore. Beat it!

3. Look over the list of phrases below. Working together, *circle* the phrases kids might say that would make worry *weaker*, and put an X through the phrases that would make worry grow *stronger*.

   - "I hear you talking, worry, but I'm going to ignore you right now."
   - "Thanks for checking in, worry, but I can handle this without you."
   - "You're right, worry, I think it's better if I don't even try that."
   - "I don't know what's going to happen, worry, so let's just stop now."
   - "Worry, you say the same things all the time, and it's getting boring!"
   - "If I put you in charge of me, worry, I won't learn how to do this."
   - "Worry *always* helps me, so I have to listen to it."

4. Role-play with your child. Learn how worry might talk and how one could respond to it.

   - First, you start off playing the role of worry and let your child talk to you.
   - Need an idea? Pretend that worry doesn't want your child to [insert favorite family activity here].
   - Then switch roles. Let your child be worry, and use the same activity again.
   - Then practice with other favorite family activities. Only use examples of activities that your child currently has no problems with.

5. Work on the skill of differentiating "sensible worry" from "bossy worry." (You may choose to use different terms.) Together, come up with examples of each. Here are a few to get you started:

Sensible Worry (good advice)	Bossy Worry (anxious advice)
Wear a helmet when you ride your bike.	Don't ride your bike! You might fall!
Wash your hands when you use the bathroom.	Wash your hands every chance you get because you could get sick.
Have a meet-up spot in case you get separated at the amusement park.	Don't go to the amusement park because you might get lost.

CHAPTER 6:
BECOMING UNGLUED

When kids attempt to stay comfortable and certain, they cannot grow stronger. When parents continually provide certainty and offer crutches for security, they strengthen anxiety's grip on families. Trust us: We know that instructing anxious kids to seek out discomfort flies in the face of how they currently negotiate through life. In this chapter we do our best to persuade your child to adopt this new stance: when you are willing to *tolerate* discomfort and to *not know* exactly what's going to happen next, you step into new territory and learn.

Casey illustrates the value of accepting doubt and discomfort through stories of daring Mount Everest ascents and the persistent inventors of Post-it Notes. She tells of people who understand that "not knowing" is an integral part of learning how to move forward. If they always played it safe, they would never make amazing discoveries or accomplish great feats. When kids tolerate not knowing, they get the chance to discover the fun of a sleepover or accomplish the feat of hitting a Little League pitch.

Reviewing Chapter 6 with Your Child

Questions to Discuss with Your Child

1. What is the "bizarre" suggestion that Casey makes in the first part of this chapter? Why does she suggest you do such a thing?
2. What are some of the ways we might feel when we are experimenting with new challenges or unfamiliar situations?
3. What did Arthur Fry do with Spencer Silver's not-so-sticky adhesive?

4. What did Erik Weihenmayer achieve? What are some of the discomforts he experienced?

5. In order to move into new territory and take control of worry, what does Casey want you to say? (Hint: It starts with "I'm *willing*...")

6. What's the formula for courage?

7. What made each of the kids—Casey, Elliot, and Kate—feel uncertain and uncomfortable? How did each of them handle their worries?

Chapter 6 Activities with Your Child

1. With your child, search history or current events or your own family for stories of people who moved into uncertainty, took risks, or tolerated discomfort in order to achieve something. As you talk about these stories, imagine together what each person had to say to himself or herself in order to keep going.

2. Create a poster, banner, kitchen magnet, index card, or other item with this formula for courage and post it visibly in your home. Perhaps your child might want to write it down and carry it to school. On a regular basis (at dinner, during car rides, at bedtime), talk together about activities you participated in each day that followed this formula.

Courage
Be willing to feel unsure
+
Be willing to feel uncomfortable
+
Step into the unknown

CHAPTER 7:
TAKING YOUR BRAIN FOR A WALK

Few children (and not too many adults) have ever been given an explanation of how anxiety is triggered in the brain and how the body then responds. This chapter helps your child understand *why* stepping toward discomfort and uncertainty is necessary, and how to implement a series of different, more courageous strategies that will retrain the brain. She introduces the third piece of the puzzle: BE UNSURE AND UNCOMFORTABLE ON PURPOSE.

Casey uses a dog named Butch as an example of how to practice these skills. He barks too much at other dogs when he goes for walks. To retrain Butch, you must take him for lots of walks. In the same way, if a child feels nervous walking into the cafeteria at school, he has to walk in anyway, bringing his amygdala with him, and talking to it in a different way. Over and over again. Change requires persistence *and* action.

Reviewing Chapter 7 with Your Child

Questions to Discuss with Your Child

1. What is the third puzzle piece?

2. What shape is your amygdala? What does it do?

3. How do you retrain your amygdala? Why is this like taking Butch for a walk?

4. What might kids say or think that will turn on their alarm centers (their amygdalae)?

5. What are the three messages Casey wants you to try out so that you can handle new challenges without pressing the danger button?

   a. I'm willing to _____.

   b. I'm willing to _____.

   c. I'm willing to _____.

6. Why does Casey want you to participate in activities that make you feel uncomfortable and uncertain?

Chapter 7 Activities with Your Child

Together, come up with four examples of events where kids or adults might feel anxiety or fear. List them below and then complete the two other columns of the form. (Stay away from activities that are anxiety-provoking for your child.)

Events Where We Might Become Afraid

Triggering event	What could you say to set off the amygdala?	What could you day to start retraining your brain?

Here is how one example might look:

Triggering event	What could you say to set off the amygdala?	What could you say to start retraining your brain?
Thunderstorms	*Thunderstorms are terrible. I can't stand them. I have to hide right now. This is bad!*	*I can handle this storm, even though it's loud, and that scares me. If I stand here in the living room and pay attention on purpose, my brain will learn, even if I feel nervous and scared.*

CHAPTER 8:
I SAY UNCOMFORTABLE,
YOU SAY VOMIT

As Casey pushes herself into new and challenging situations, she discovers that at times her alarm system threatens to go off. Through a variety of experiences—on a roller coaster, at a running race, with a pencil—she learns that she can reset and gain control with a quick focus on her breathing and her muscles. This increases her confidence and supports her clear thinking. She teaches the reader two specific skills for brief relaxation within this fourth puzzle piece: *BREATHE!* The extra bonus of these skills? It's impossible to be freaked out and relaxed at the same time!

Reviewing Chapter 8 with Your Child

Questions to Discuss with Your Child

1. What is the fourth puzzle piece?

2. When Casey rode the roller coaster, she didn't turn on her alarm system. How did she keep it turned off? What did she notice about her friend Lindsay?

3. Casey learned a trick with a pencil. What was the purpose of the trick? (Try this with your child.)

4. Why does Casey want kids to practice the skills when they're not anxious?

5. How does Casey's friend Bridget handle herself at the cross-country meet?

6. What does Casey do differently at the cross-country meet?

Chapter 8 Activities with Your Child

Keep in mind that the breathing skills described below can be practiced simply and quickly and that repetition is important. A few Calming Breaths multiple times throughout the day will take a total of less than five minutes.

1. Make a list of the different feelings possible in the body when someone is nervous (sweaty palms, increased heart rate, etc.). Interview other adults or family members about how their bodies feel when they're nervous.

2. Practice the Calming Breath and Calming Counts with your child. (They were first described in Chapter 8 of this book.) Younger children need to learn through modeling, so practice these skills together at first. Older children and teens will be able to manage

on their own rather quickly. Teach the skills in a quiet setting
without interruption. After you both have practiced several times
over several days, incorporate the skills into your everyday routine. Set a goal of practicing these simple breathing "resets" at
least three times a day. Moments of transition are good opportunities: at a stoplight, in the car, at the beginning of a meal, at the
dinner table, before diving into homework, or even between math
problems. You can post little helpful reminders around the house
or in the car.

Calming Breath

1. Breathe out all the way.
2. Take a deep breath in, letting your belly expand first,
    and then your chest.
3. Slowly exhale, saying "calm" (or a similar word) under
    your breath. (We like "okay," or sometimes "fine." Keep
    it simple.)
4. Let your muscles go limp and warm; loosen your face
    and jaw muscles.
5. Remain in this "resting" position for a few more
    seconds, without thinking about your breathing or
    anything else.

Calming Counts

1. Breathe out all the way.
2. Take a deep breath in, letting your belly expand first, and then your chest.
3. Slowly exhale, saying "calm" (or some other simple word) under your breath.
4. Now take ten gentle, easy breaths, while you silently count down with each exhale, starting with 10.
5. At the same time, invite the muscles in your jaw or forehead or stomach to loosen. Imagine them loosening.

Simply focus on taking ten easy, loose, gentle breaths that give a calming message to your entire body and brain. While counting down and getting loose, feel free to smile. Breathe. Loosen. Smile.

It's important that they begin practice during times when they *aren't* feeling anxious. The skills should be well-rehearsed, ready to go when needed. We can predict that if your child is not familiar with these skills through her repeated practice, then when you suggest she use them as she becomes anxious or panicky, she won't find them helpful or she'll refuse to try them at all.

3. To give your child the experience of controlling her physical reactions, you can play games with increasing and decreasing pulse rates.

- First, take your child's pulse; for older children, show them how to do it on their own. If you've never done it before, here are some simple instructions: Place the index and middle finger on the inside of the wrist. Your fingers should be right below the wrist crease and near the thumb. You can also use the carotid artery at the neck. This is located below the ear, on the side of the neck directly below the jaw.
- As soon as you feel a pulse, count the pulse beats for fifteen seconds (you'll need a watch).
- Multiply the number you get by 4. This gives you the individual's heartbeats per minute, or pulse rate.
- Take a starting pulse.
- Then have your child do a physical activity for a minute or two, like jumping jacks, skipping, or running up and down a flight of stairs.
- When they stop, take the pulse again. (It should be much higher!)
- Then, practice three Calming Breaths in a row with about ten to fifteen seconds' break between each one. Or try Calming Counts.
- Take the pulse rate again. (It should be much lower.) Continue playing with the breathing skills until the heart rate is back to (or very close to) the original rate.
- Suggest that whenever worry scares them unnecessarily, their hearts will probably beat faster, too. It's *supposed* to. Practicing the breathing skills can help decrease their heart rates as long as they don't keep turning on their alarm systems with more worries.

CHAPTER 9:
WRESTLING WITH ASPARAGUS

The next piece of the puzzle is KNOW WHAT YOU WANT. Casey meets Benjamin, who tells his own story of overcoming worry. She realizes that it's a lot easier to overcome a difficult step if you choose an exciting or important goal. Casey illustrates how to identify each of the steps toward a desired goal. The message is consistent: move forward into the challenge, equipped with the new tools you are developing, a goal you're interested in, and the "I can handle this" voice.

Examples within this chapter are spending time at a friend's house, jumping from a Coast Guard helicopter, and eating an asparagus-dog with cheese.

Reviewing Chapter 9 with Your Child

Questions to Discuss with Your Child

1. Do you remember what Benjamin's goal was?
2. When he thought about going over to someone else's house, what were some of the events he was afraid of?
3. What was Uncle Steve's goal? And what was he afraid of?
4. Uncle Steve sounded like he was pretty scared. If he was so afraid, why *did* he keep pushing?
5. What did Uncle Steve decide to do with his worry? Did he leave it behind or take it with him? What did he say to it?
6. What was the vegetable that Casey was having trouble with? Why did she have to eat it? How'd she get herself to eat it? (Consider going step-by-step through the text regarding how Casey got to the neighborhood meeting.)

Chapter 9 Activities with Your Child

1. Review together Casey's tips for creating and using the want-to attitude. Converse easily about this topic; let your child talk about it freely, even expressing doubt. Be open to her opinion. Encourage (and model) the ability to ponder questions and problem solve. We recommend that you apply this concept to activities that are *not* directly related to your child's major fears.

2. Each of you choose a chore that you don't much like but do anyway (emptying the dishwasher, putting away the laundry, cleaning out the car, doing math homework, etc.).

   a. What could you say to yourself that would make the job *harder* to complete?

   b. What could you say to yourself, or what could you do, that would make the chore easier, quicker, or more enjoyable?

3. The next time you or your child begin a not-so-exciting chore, talk to each other about how you could approach the task to make it feel harder. Then follow Casey's strategy of approaching the task in a way that makes it more interesting, easier, or quicker. Casey gave the example of cleaning up her bedroom by turning it into a game.

   Here's an example of how it might sound:

   > I really don't like to empty the dishwasher.
   >
   > If I want to make it *harder* and *even more annoying*:
   >
   > I can tell myself how long it takes, and how I HATE doing it, and how I HAVE to do it every day, even though I don't want to. Maybe I can think about the part that I find the most tedious . . . putting the silverware away in the drawer. [Feel free to be silly.] Or I can make myself hop on one foot as I carry each dish to the shelf.

> If I want it to be *easier*:
>
> I can tell myself that emptying the dishwasher makes room for all the dirty dishes, and when the counters and sink are clean and clear, it looks much nicer. I can also remind myself that it only takes a few minutes, and I might even time myself just to see how fast I can get it done. Maybe I can empty the silverware first, to get it out of the way.

4. Together with your child, ask others for examples that demonstrate the logic of wanting (and doing) something unpleasant in order to reach a goal. How do they turn an unpleasant event into a tolerable one? How do they get around to accomplishing the task when they don't feel like it? Find at least three different examples. In addition to hearing a range of interesting illustrations, there is an important added benefit here. As your child interviews others, she first has to explain the principle of the puzzle piece. That helps her incorporate it into her logical reasoning.

5. Generate a few routine, everyday examples of how each of you makes a common (but not very exciting or pleasant) task more manageable in your own lives. How do you get tasks done? What do you say to yourself when it's time to clean the cat litter? How do you willingly go to the dentist regularly? If you find examples where you don't say or do *anything* to tolerate the project, what *could* you say or do?

6. Create a hypothetical goal for you, your child, or even a character in a book. It can be silly, outrageous, or fun. (For now, resist tackling an event that is closely connected to your child's specific worries. At this point, we're teaching the skills in a nonthreatening way.)

- What steps must you take to get to that goal?
- How can you talk to yourself if you want to make that goal seem harder? What might you say that would make you want to give up?
- What could you say and do that would make you excited to tackle the goal? What could you do that would make you want to get started? Here's how it might sound:

I have a goal of making the world's biggest meatball. First, I have to find out what the current record is. Then, I need a huge kitchen to use, and a recipe to tell me how much meat and other ingredients to buy at the store. And I must save up my allowance to afford it all. I have to find some friends to help and make sure I have a scale and some officials there to take the measurements.

If I wanted to *discourage* myself, I could tell myself that breaking such a record is too much work, and I won't be able to do it anyway. I might tell myself that only chefs make big meatballs, so why waste time trying?

If I wanted to *inspire* myself, I could remind myself that all records are broken by following a plan, one step at a time. I might think about how great I'd feel if I actually do it. And they'd probably write about my accomplishment in the paper! Maybe I'd say, "This is going to be tiring, and hot, and challenging, but that feeling of victory will be worth it, and my friends and I will have some great fun and stories to tell in the end!"

CHAPTER 10:
CHUTES AND LEARNERS

W orry makes you forget. That's why a worried kid can get on the bus for sixty-five school days in a row, do fine sixty-five times, and still be afraid on day sixty-six. In this chapter, Casey explains another piece of the puzzle: BRIDGE BACK TO YOUR SUCCESSES, which explains the importance of learning from experience. Telling her own story of unrelenting worry about schoolwork, Casey shows how to remember and reference positive experiences from the past and how to make those experiences count toward the "I can handle this" attitude.

Stories include perfectionism at school, Casey's mom coping with the stresses of new motherhood, handling the fear of bees and the fear of flying, and trying out for the school musical.

Reviewing Chapter 10 with Your Child

Questions to Discuss with Your Child

1. What do you imagine Erik Weihenmayer learned that helped him climb some challenging mountains? If you were a mountain climber, what mistakes might you make as a beginner? What would you do differently the next time?

2. Casey's mom and Mrs. O'Shea kept telling Casey that she was a great student and learner, but Casey stayed frustrated. Why didn't their words help?

3. What are some of the bridges that Casey's mom built? How did they help?

4. Casey and Lindsay both have the same thought when they see a bee: "I hope I don't get stung!" But after that, their thoughts move

in different directions. What does Lindsay think about bees? And what do those thoughts make her do? How does Casey handle her bee thoughts? What does she do to handle the bees?

Chapter 10 Activities with Your Child

1. Find examples when you have each used a mental bridge back to your past successes as a way to encourage yourself to move into an uncomfortable new situation. Help your child ask other adults as well. Use this form to write down the events:

Examples of Bridging Back to Success

I really wanted to . . .	That reminded me of how . . .	That reminded me how I could handle . . .
Bake Emma's birthday cake from scratch	*I made my own tortillas for the first time, and they turned out better than I imagined.*	*Making a "good enough" birthday cake, even if it wasn't as pretty as a store-bought one.*

2. As we near the end of the puzzle pieces, conduct a little review of situations that tend to provoke worry. Using the worry triggers listed below, come up with examples that fit each of the situations. Ask other adults and siblings, or think about favorite characters in books. Or make stuff up! (Remember to avoid bringing up your child's emotionally loaded, worry-provoking topics . . . but if your child brings them up, you can talk about how you both might handle such situations.)

Here's the list of times when worry tends to show up (from Chapter 4 of *Casey's Guide*):

- You're doing some new or different activity.
- You're unsure about your plans.
- You have a lot of "what if" questions.
- You have to perform.
- Something scary is happening.

Here's how it might sound:

> You may feel worried on the first day of school or if you're starting a new job. [doing some new or different activity]
>
> Worry might show up if you're traveling in a new city and looking for a good place to eat dinner, and you're not sure where to go. [unsure about plans]
>
> Remember when Casey felt worried about the thunderstorm at the water park? She asked a lot of questions. What if it rains? What if the party is cancelled? ["what if" questions]
>
> Uncle Sam told me he was nervous before he sang at his friend's wedding last year. But he did it! [performance]
>
> Gram told me she was driving on a snowy road one winter and her car started sliding on the ice. She said her heart was beating fast and her hands were shaking like crazy. [scary stuff]

3. Put the puzzle pieces together. Review with your child what you have learned in previous chapters. The more he explores and discusses the principles, the greater the chance he has of applying them.

    -   Kids and parents should expect worry to show up when trying and learning new things. (expect to worry) *See Chapter 4 for a reminder, if needed.*
    -   Kids and parents can confront worry, rather than listening to it and believing what it says. (talk to worry) *See Chapter 5 for a reminder, if needed.*
    -   Moving forward into new activities means you'll feel uncomfortable and uncertain. That's normal, and it's how we learn from the experiences of life. Kids need to get uncomfortable *on purpose*, because practice and exposure, rather than avoidance, help kids learn how to handle new activities. (get uncomfortable on purpose) *See Chapter 7 for a reminder, if needed.*
    -   Knowing how to quiet the brain's alarm system increases confidence as kids move forward with their practice. (breathe!) *See Chapter 8 for a reminder, if needed.*
    -   Focusing on a goal helps you move forward. If you want to grow in life, you need to push into new territory. If you focus on your uncomfortable feelings, you'll stop. If you focus on getting where you want to go, you'll still have feelings, of course, and some of them will be unpleasant, but the steps will be easier because they will be a part of your want-to. This way you send your brain *one* consistent message: "I want this outcome, so I'm willing to take the not-so-easy steps along the way to get it." (know what you want) *See Chapter 9 for a reminder, if needed.*

CHAPTER 11:
ANSWERING THE BELL

A t last, the plan in action! Elliot arrives home from school one day, refusing to go back because of the scary fire drills. Mom, Casey, and Elliot team up to make a plan and then *take action on their plan* (the last puzzle piece) that allows Elliot to use his thinking, his breathing, and his past experiences to manage the startling and unpleasant noise. The pieces of the puzzle are assembled now, and with them Elliot steps into the situation and handles the fire drills.

Stories include Elliot managing the school fire drills and Casey's family coming across a snake on their camping trip.

Reviewing Chapter 11 with Your Child

Questions to Discuss with Your Child

1. What did Elliot want to do about the school fire drills at first? Why did Mom disagree with this plan?

2. What did Elliot, Casey, and Mom do when they first came upon the snake while hiking? What did they do next? How did remembering the snake incident help Elliot with his plan to handle fire drills?

3. How did Casey and Elliot practice for the fire drills?

4. What did Elliot do at school when there was a fire drill? What did he tell himself to get through it?

Chapter 11 Activities with Your Child

Below is "Casey's Really Clever Guide to Winning over Worries."

Know what you want to accomplish.
Remember your past successes that can help you.
Expect worry to show up.
Talk to your worries so they can't run the show.
Step into that new situation.
Be willing to feel unsure and uncomfortable along the way.
Let your breathing skills support you.

These are the seven puzzle pieces, put in a new sequence. Using the puzzle pieces, come up with a fictional goal—even a silly activity, along the lines of building the world's biggest meatball (from the activities in Chapter 9)—and use the puzzle pieces as your guide to move step by step toward the goal. If the want-to is to build a spaceship, for example, and you've never done that before, you can expect worry to show up. What will it say? What will you say to it? Do you have any other successes that you can remember as you build? When might you need to stop and breathe along the way? What makes you feel uncomfortable or uncertain about building a spaceship? What will you do to handle those feelings?

Examples to Help Spark Your Creativity

- Build a spaceship.
- Learn to ride an elephant.
- Live in the jungle.
- Make a giant snowman.

CHAPTER 12:
THE SHOW MUST GO ON!

Casey and friend Shannon both want to be involved in the school musical. Then the worries show up, along with second thoughts and doubts. Another chance to work the plan! Again with Mom's help, the girls use the pieces of the puzzle as a guide to come up with their own plans. By applying the strategies, they let themselves feel uncomfortable, tolerate uncertainty, take plenty of deep breaths, and have a great time reaching their goals.

Reviewing Chapter 12 with Your Child

1. What activity did Casey and Shannon hear about at school?

2. When Casey and Shannon are home from school eating potato chips, what does worry start to say to them?

3. Casey realizes that this is another chance to practice her plan, so her mom prints out some worksheets and they get to work. What is Shannon's goal? How will Shannon practice her worry-managing skills?

4. What unexpected things happen to Shannon and Casey during rehearsals and the performances?

5. Do you think Casey and Shannon enjoyed the experience of the play? What did they learn about handling worry and trying something new?

Anxiety Disorders
Diagnosed in Childhood
or Adolescence

The following are the major anxiety disorders that can be diagnosed in childhood or adolescence.* Note that health professionals do not diagnose a disorder based only on the symptoms present. The disturbance caused by the disorder must result in *significant distress or impairment* in the child's routine, school functioning, family functioning, and social relationships.

SEPARATION ANXIETY DISORDER (SAD)

This disorder identifies excessive anxiety regarding separation from home or from specific individuals. Consider the possibility of

---

* Adapted from *Diagnostic and Statistical Manual of Mental Disorders, Fifth Edition*, American Psychiatric Association, 2013.

separation anxiety disorder if the child exhibits three or more of the following:

- Repeated distress because of separation or the possibility of separation from home or a specific individual, like a parent
- Worry about losing an important person, or some harm coming to them
- Worry that an event would cause separation (like getting lost or being kidnapped)
- Refusing to go to school or to other activities out of fear of separation
- Difficulty being alone
- Difficulty going to sleep without an important person close by, or difficulty sleeping away from home
- Nightmares about separation
- Complaints of physical symptoms because of separation or the possibility of separation

GENERALIZED ANXIETY DISORDER

This disorder identifies excessive, uncontrollable worry about a variety of topics. Topics of the worry can include their performance or competence in school or sporting events, punctuality, or catastrophic events like an earthquake. Their worries can focus on the past, present, and/or future. These children or adolescents can be perfectionistic, self-doubting, and approval- or reassurance-seeking. The diagnosis requires at least one of these symptoms associated with the worry: restlessness, tiredness, poor concentration, irritability, muscle tension, or poor sleep.

SPECIFIC PHOBIA

This disorder identifies excessive fear in the presence of or in anticipation of a specific object or situation. Common phobias in children are dogs, injections, thunderstorms, flying, heights, the dark, blood, and vomiting. The object can only be endured with intense distress, commonly expressed by crying, tantrums, or clinging behaviors. However, the most frequent coping mechanism in specific phobias is avoidance.

SOCIAL ANXIETY DISORDER

This disorder identifies children who fear appearing foolish or acting in a way that would be criticized or ridiculed by others. They actively seek to avoid being humiliated or embarrassed in one or more social or performance situations, such as parties, talking to authority figures, or speaking to others in public. The diagnosis requires that this fear occur not only in the presence of adults but in peer situations as well. Symptoms may include crying, tantrums, and freezing. The most common coping mechanism is avoidance.

OBSESSIVE-COMPULSIVE DISORDER (OCD)

This disorder identifies children who experience recurring, uncontrollable, unwanted thoughts, impulses, or images that produce intense anxiety or distress. These obsessions are not focused on real-life problems. Common obsessions relate to contamination, doubting oneself, needing to have things in a particular order, or aggressive impulses. In an attempt to reduce distress or prevent something bad from happening, the child or teen engages in compulsions: rigid, repetitive behaviors or mental processes. Common compulsions (also called "rituals") include excessive hand washing, checking, counting, repeating words or prayers silently, or seeking frequent reassurance from others.

PANIC DISORDER

This disorder identifies children who experience recurrent, unexpected panic attacks. The sudden rush of uncomfortable physical sensations may include difficulty breathing, dizziness, abdominal discomfort, and racing heart. The intense, fearful thoughts relate to an immediate personal threat, such as "I can't breathe," "I'm going crazy," or "I'm going to die." Over at least a one-month period, the child will worry about additional attacks and may begin to avoid any behavior or situations that might provoke an additional attack.

POST-TRAUMATIC STRESS DISORDER (PTSD)

This disorder identifies children who are struggling for at least one month after experiencing or witnessing a traumatic event that involved actual or threatened death or severe injury, such as a car accident or robbery. The child responds with intense fear, helplessness, or disorganized or agitated behavior. Reexperiencing of the trauma occurs in any one of several ways: intrusive memories of the event; repetitive play that includes themes of the trauma; frightening dreams, whether or not associated with the event; and feeling as though the trauma is occurring again. The child avoids stimulus associated with the trauma, including thoughts, feelings, places, activities, and conversations. Such children may also feel numb, detached, and a sense that their life is shortened, as though they will never grow up to be an adult. Symptoms of anxiety can include difficulty sleeping, angry outbursts, poor concentration, vigilance, and an exaggerated startle response.

National Organizations That Identify Therapists Specializing in the Treatment of Anxiety

Each of these organizations offers an online search function that identifies therapists who work specifically with anxiety disorders. They also allow you to limit your search to those who treat children or adolescents.

Anxiety and Depression Association of America
www.adaa.org

International OCD Foundation
www.ocfoundation.org

Association for Behavioral and Cognitive Therapies
www.abct.org

American Psychological Association
www.apa.org

Children's Books That Model Healthy Cognitive Styles

There are hundreds of wonderful children's books that illustrate the skills children (and the parents who read aloud to them) can use to manage anxious moments, develop flexibility, and revel in the unexpected moments of growing up. This list of books is meant to be a starting point.

UP TO AGE 5

Not a Box by Antoinette Portis (HarperCollins, 2007)

A bunny shows that he won't be boxed in by a box. Teaches kids: imagination, versatility, thinking outside the box.

The Carrot Seed by Ruth Krauss, ill. by Crockett Johnson (HarperCollins, 2004)

A classic, simple, sweet tale of internal persistence in the face of grown-up doubt. Teaches kids: confidence, persistence, determination, positive expectancy.

Yahoo for You by Dana Meachen Rau, ill. by Cary Pillo
(Compass Point Books, 2006)

This book offers a direct and simple message to little ones about trying new things. Teaches kids: flexibility, risk taking, exploring.

Brave, Brave Mouse by Michaela Morgan, ill. by Michelle Cartlidge (Albert Whitman & Company, 2004)

A mouse learns how and when to say yes, and that no works, too, sometimes. Teaches kids: selectivity, discrimination, the good combination of risks and limits.

We'll All Go Exploring by Maggee Spicer and Richard Thompson, ill. by Kim Lafave (Fitzhenry and Whiteside, 2003)

Supports the simple joys of exploring the world around us. Teaches kids: exploring, investigating.

Make It Change by David Evans and Claudette Williams
(Dorling Lindersley Publishers Ltd., 1992)

A science book for children, with simple experiments that promote the thinking *and* the doing. Teaches kids: experimenting, change happens, taking action, cause and effect.

AGE 4 AND UP

The Owl Who Was Afraid of the Dark by Jill Tomlinson and Paul Howard (Egmont UK, 2004)

Plop the owl learns to see darkness as less scary when he experiences it from others' perspectives. (There are several other books in this series with titles like *The Hen Who Wouldn't Give Up*.) Teaches kids: flexibility, shifts in perspective, experience is malleable.

Time of Wonder by Robert McCloskey (Viking Press, 1968)

Children experience (safely) a hurricane on their beloved Maine island, and then discover how the landscape changes in interesting ways. Teaches kids: adaptability, change happens, shifts in perspective, flexibility.

Once Upon an Ordinary School Day by Colin McNaughton, ill. by Satoshi Kitamura (Farrar, Straus and Giroux, 2005)

A regular school day takes some unexpected turns in this wonderful, magical book. Teaches kids: imagination, possibilities, thinking outside the box, positive expectancy.

Begin at the Beginning: A Little Artist Learns about Life by Amy Schwartz (Katherine Tegen Books, 2005)

An overwhelmed little girl learns how to make a big challenge manageable. Teaches kids: steps and sequencing, accessing resources.

Something Might Happen by Helen Lester, ill. by Lynn Musinger (Houghton Mifflin Books for Children, 2003)

Yep. Something might. Teaches kids: how to manage the unknown, experimentation, discovering and accessing resources.

The Summerfolk by Doris Burns (Weekly Reader Book Club Edition, 1968)

A shy, isolated, grumpy boy meets a unique cadre of children, and has a good time in spite of himself . . . a favorite from Lynn's childhood that delights even after thousands of readings. Teaches kids: malleability of experience, flexibility, shifting perspectives, social skills, risk taking.

Wanda's Monster by Eileen Spinelli, ill. by Nancy Hayashi
(Albert Whitman and Company, 2002)

Wanda learns of a whole new way to handle a monster in the closet, and learns that worries come, but then go, too. Teaches kids: worries and fears are manageable and malleable, shifting perspectives, creativity, and accessing resources.

Beverly Billingsly Takes a Bow by Alexander Stadler
(Harcourt Children's Books, 2002)

Beverly gets hesitantly into the action and discovers that good things happen when you put yourself in the game, just sometimes not how you expect. Teaches kids: flexibility, discovery, the ability to create a happy ending, the need to take action.

Beverly Billingsly Borrows a Book by Alexander Stadler
(Harcourt Children's Books, 2003)

Beverly shows how problems can get bigger in your imagination. This one shows avoidance in action. Teaches kids: that action helps more than ruminating and avoidance, the pitfalls of jumping to conclusions, sometimes solutions are simple.

Sally Jean, the Bicycle Queen by Carl Best, ill. by Christine Davenier (Farrar, Straus and Giroux, 2006)

Sally Jean grows into and out of her beloved bicycles, while solving many conundrums along the way. Teaches kids: persistence, creativity, resourcefulness, steps and sequencing, mastery.

Fortunately by Remy Charlip (Perfection Learning, 2010)

What happens when you're invited to a birthday party thousands of miles away? You figure out how to get there! Teaches kids: resourcefulness, hopefulness, persistence.

A Friend Like Ed by Karen Wagner and Janet Pedersen
(Orchard/Watts Group, 2000)

Ed is a bit eccentric, and Mildred goes in search of a more "normal" friend, only to return to Ed, kookiness and all. Teaches kids: accepting differences, loyalty, flexibility, the importance and possibility of connection and friendship.

Watching . . . by Suzy Chic and Monique Toursay
(WingedChariot Press, 2007)

A sweet little book about patience and the joys of letting things unfold in their own time. Teaches kids: patience, planning, the opposite of impulsivity, generosity, sequencing.

The Frog and Toad Books Collection Box Set
by Arnold Lobel (HarperCollins, 2004)

The classic read-aloud stories, all with a moral worthy of discussion. Wonderfully, sweetly written. Teaches kids: all sorts of great things about friendship and bravery and flexibility and kindness.

Ming Lo Moves the Mountain by Arnold Lobel (Scholastic, 1986)

Ming Lo and his wife want to move the mountain away from their house but discover that a change in perspective offers the same happy result. There's more than one way to move a mountain! Teaches kids: flexibility, creativity, problem solving.

Fables by Arnold Lobel (HarperCollins, 1980)

More tales from Mr. Lobel, with fresh and funny morals and wonderful illustrations. Teaches kids: flexibility, risk taking, the power of observation, the dangers of getting stuck.

Beetle McGrady Eats Bugs by Megan McDonald
(Greenwillow Books, 2005)

Beetle McGrady is a daring girl who takes on the challenge of eating bugs, just to show she can. This will make picky eaters squirm, but Beetle's determination in the face of her cautious classmates is contagious. Teaches kids: persistence, experimenting, risk taking.

The Opposite by Tom MacRae and Elena Odriozola
(Peachtree Pub Ltd., 2006)

This is a brilliant book that describes how every anxious kid should tackle the part inside that holds him or her back. We wish we had written this book and are very glad we came across it. Teaches kids: the critical concept of confronting anxiety and fear rather than avoiding.

ACKNOWLEDGMENTS

The principles of this book, and its companion guide for and kids, reflect our studies throughout our entire careers. So many clinicians and clinician-researchers have worked tirelessly to contribute to our understanding of children and families with anxiety. We express our appreciation to all of these professionals, including: Anne Marie Albano, PhD, Phil Nendall, PhD, Danny Pine, MD, John Piacentini, PhD, John Walkup, MD, John March, MD, Aureen Wagner, PhD, Karen Cassiday, PhD, Tom Ollendick, PhD, Golda Ginsburg, PhD, Tamar Chansky, PhD, Ronald Rapee, PhD, Lynn Siqueland, PhD, Paula Barrett, PhD, Jerome Kagan, PhD, Eric Storch, PhD, Cynthia Last, PhD, Jill Ehrenreich May, PhD, and Candice A. Alfano, PhD.

We are so grateful for those who have supported our work over the years: Michael Yapko, PhD, Jeffrey Zeig, PhD, Alan Konell, MSW, Jack Hirose, PhD, Paul Ortman, Dan Barmettler, PhD, Rich Simon, PhD, and Alies Muskin, MA. Special thanks to Carol Mann, our agent.

Especially from Lynn: Michael Yapko has been the most inspiring and encouraging of mentors, and I hope he doesn't tire of hearing me saying thank you. Luckily I met Jay Essif early enough in my career to make all the difference. I am grateful to Mark, Ruth, Hank, Jeff, Virginia, Peter, and all my Rigmor pals for being so smart, so warm, and so supportive; and to Christine, the truest example of exactly what a friend should be. I am surrounded by a family that is loving, curious, funny, and resilient. I thank my parents, Ed and Cathleen, and Nancy, Ed, and Robin for their limitless love, encouragement, and humor. Crawford, Zed, and Brackett make my life better every day. And, finally, thank you to Reid for having an idea, taking a chance, and asking me to write a book with him.

HOW TO FIND CASEY'S GUIDE

In *Playing with Anxiety: Casey's Guide for Teens and Kids*, fourteen-year-old Casey tells the story of her struggle with anxiety and her discovery of seven strategies that changed her life. With tales of roller coasters, fire drills, slimy asparagus, and helicopters, Casey engages kids and teens with humor, encouragement, and a solid plan for action. Parents and younger children can read together, while teens can learn independently. The benefit? Two books that give all family members a common language and a successful strategy to win over worry. Download the free e-book at: *www.PlayingWith Anxiety.com*.

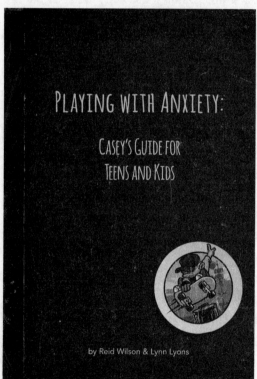

PLAYING WITH ANXIETY:

CASEY'S GUIDE FOR
TEENS AND KIDS

by Reid Wilson & Lynn Lyons

A SNEAK PEEK AT CASEY'S GUIDE FOR TEENS AND KIDS

by Reid Wilson, PhD & Lynn Lyons, LICSW

CONTENTS

ABOUT THE AUTHORS

REID WILSON, PhD, is Director of the Anxiety Disorders Treatment Center in Chapel Hill and Durham, North Carolina, and is Associate Clinical Professor of Psychiatry at the University of North Carolina School of Medicine. Dr. Wilson is an international expert in the treatment of anxiety disorders, with books translated into nine languages. He is author of the classic self-help book, *Don't Panic: Taking Control of Anxiety Attacks,* now in its third edition (Harper), as well as *Facing Panic: Self-Help for People with Panic Attacks (ADAA).* Dr. Wilson is co-author with Lynn Lyons of the free ebook, *Playing with Anxiety: Casey's Guide for Teens and Kids (PlayingWithAnxiety.com).* He is also co-author with Dr. Edna Foa of *Stop Obsessing! How to Overcome Your Obsessions and Compulsions* (Bantam) and co-author with Captain Slim Cummings of *Achieving Comfortable Flight,* a self-help package for the fearful flier. His new video series, Strategic Treatment of the Anxiety Disorders, includes *Exposure Therapy for Phobias, Cognitive Therapy for Obsessions, Cognitive Therapy for Panic Disorder, Engaging the Ambivalent OCD Client,* and *Treating the Severe OCD Client.* This series is published in both DVD and video streaming format by Psychotherapy.net. He currently serves as the Expert for WebMD's Anxiety and Panic Community. He designed and served as lead psychologist for American Airlines' first national program for the fearful flier. Dr. Wilson served on the Board of Directors of the Anxiety Disorders Association of America for twelve years. He served as Program Chair of the National Conferences on Anxiety Disorders from 1988 to 1991. His free self-help website, anxieties.com, serves 156,000 visitors per year. He is a member of the 2003 Vanguard (first) Class of Certified Graduates of Dr. Martin Seligman's Authentic Happiness Coaching Program. He's been teaching about positive psychology principles since then.

Television appearances include *The Oprah Winfrey Show*, *Good Morning America*, CNN, CNN-Financial Network, A&E's *Hoarders* and various local news shows across the nation.

LYNN LYONS, LICSW, has been a psychotherapist for over twenty-three years and specializes in the treatment of anxious children and their parents, with a particular interest in interrupting the generational patterns of anxiety in families. In addition to her private practice in Concord, New Hampshire, Lynn presents internationally to professional organizations and school districts, offering workshops to mental health and medical providers, teachers, school nurses, and parents. She is known for her focus on providing concrete, usable skills and her integration of humor, homework, and clinical hypnosis.

She is the coauthor of *Anxious Kids, Anxious Parents: 7 Ways to Stop the Worry Cycle and Raise Courageous and Independent Children* and the companion book *Playing with Anxiety: Casey's Guide for Teens and Kids.* She also created a self-help DVD program for parents entitled *Decreasing Anxiety: How to Talk to Your Anxious Child.*

Remember the 7 Keys to Solving the Worry Puzzle . . .

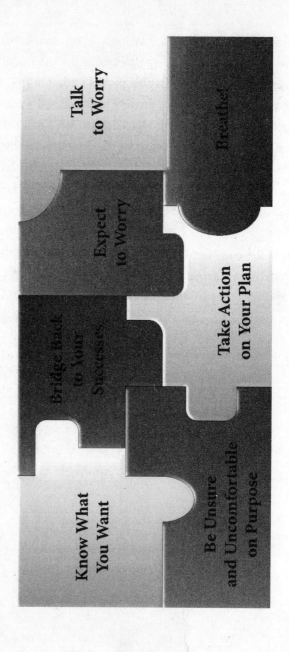